A Stroll Through Fitzgerald, GA In The Forties

Paul B.

2005

Front cover photograph depicts Fitzgerald's AB&A Railroad Passenger Depot, which now houses the Blue & Gray Museum. It is the starting point for the stroll through Fitzgerald described in this book. Photo by Steve Butler.

Back cover photo of Mr. Dunn by Ruby Hodgman.

Introduction, *A World on the Brink*, by Sherri Butler.

Cover design by Lee Clevenger and R. Preston Ward

First printing, September 2005.

ISBN Number 0-9764052-3-7

ThomasMax Publishing
P.O. Box 250054
Atlanta, GA 30325
404-794-6588
www.thomasmax.com

A World on the Brink

Few people know the city of Fitzgerald as it was in the 1930s and 1940s like Paul Dunn. Growing up in a house on Central Avenue near the heart of downtown, he roamed the streets throughout his boyhood and youth. Whether he was trying to earn a little money by selling candy on the sidewalks or taking bundles of newspapers to Nick Pope at the Greek cafe, or just playing hooky from school to hitch a ride on a drayman's wagon and pretend to drive the team, Paul was up and down the city's sidewalks and alleys, exploring its businesses and offices and listening to the tales of its citizens while he watched them work.

With a writer's curiosity and observant nature, he studied how things were done in the grownup world around him. Paul witnessed a time of profound change. From the dark days of the Great Depression through the World War II home front, to the end of the war, he saw the world of his childhood transformed into a more hectic place with new automobiles filling its streets and old ways of doing things giving way to new ones, in the workaday world and at home, too.

In this book, Paul captures a town and a way of life on the brink. Corner groceries share space with the first supermarket. A livery stable co-exists, for a little while longer, with car dealerships and auto supply stores. The ice man still chips out fifty-cent pieces of ice, while more affluent citizens pen their names to waiting lists for the next shipment of refrigerators. Spectators on the sidewalk can watch bottles cycle through the assembly line to be filled with Coca-Cola and hear the thrum of sewing machines from the upstairs windows of a pants factory up the street. The railroad is still the artery that links small-town life to a world beyond, bringing in goods, taking away raw materials and delivering families and businessmen to Atlanta for a day's adventure.

It is a world he remembers vividly and describes in telling detail in an impromptu "stroll" through the city's streets. Streets he peoples with well-remembered and beloved "town characters," letting us hear their voices and watch them work and talk. From the town's most successful business and professional people to the scissors sharpener and sidewalk jewelry seller, they are all here. In the pages of this book, in words framed by affectionate memory, Paul gives them life again.

(EDITOR'S NOTE: Native Paul Dunn grew up in downtown Fitzgerald and from his boyhood explored its streets, shops and offices. In a series of stories—the first one is below—Paul invites you to take a stroll with him into the past, to 1946 or thereabout, and stop and revisit old friends from days gone by and a way of life that has vanished. Parenthetical comments in the narrative that follows were added for clarification.)

Good morning. It is a warm spring day in the month of May, 1946. World War II has finally been won, and the boys, or should I say men, are back home and picking up the lives they had left behind. Business is good, the town is back to normal.

The morning train ran a few hours earlier. Newspapers, ice and milk have been delivered. I am at the railroad depot, sitting in the cafe that is open 24 hours a day, to greet the passengers, railroad workers, night people and "loafers" like me, here to hear the latest news and gossip. I don't know how Mrs. Sydney Hawkins, the proprietress-waitress, can put up with such a crowd.

There is "Cuff," "Jake" and "Lott," three drivers for the Blue Bird Taxi Co. Willie Cleveland has just driven up in his old Model "A" Ford roadster with the big taxi sign in the side window, after taking a fare to the St. James Hotel. The train crew that brought the passenger train from Atlanta last night is, if I am not mistaken, George Talbot, engineer, Robert Ryan, fireman, Sim Burns, conductor, George Warbington, baggage master, and Frank Eppes, flagman.

I believe that is the railroad protection detective, Henry Fountain, coming in for a cup of coffee. He is in his "suit of clothes" with his small holster on his belt, very shiny, and his small pistol snapped snugly in it.

The room, with its marble counter and metal tables and chairs, with wire legs, has witnessed many such crowds and heard many hair-raising stories of foggy nights, "headlight meets", low water in boilers, short flags, broken rails, whispered gossip and groaning laughter at shady jokes. (A "headlight meet" was when two trains on parallel tracks met each other at night. A "short flag" was when the flagman just barely had enough time to wave down an oncoming train and prevent it from running into one further down the tracks.)

The coffee, bacon, eggs and grits that were served had been ample and good. The black women who cook for Mrs. Hawkins have long white aprons, wear slippers that have been cut open to be more comfortable and smile a lot to show their gold teeth. Some drivers have left a nice tip.

I hate to leave. It is getting late. Perhaps you have an hour or so? We will just stroll up the sidewalk. We won't need an automobile. It is warm, so everyone will have their windows and doors open to greet us.

I said we are going on the sidewalk. But let's begin here on the station platform that stretches the entire block from Jackson Street to Johnson Street. We will go this way to Johnson Street so we can see the station park and the large goldfish pool surrounded by red radiance roses, so carefully tended by Ted Dunn and his agency force. I also think we should see the goldfish, as large as the mullet fish that arrived in wooden barrels, capped with crushed ice and croaker sacks, on the night train from Brunswick. By the way, the mullet are on sale, 12 cents a pound, at McCall's Fish Market on Sherman Street. That is quite high, but they are fresh.

We pass the palm trees that grow in all four corners of the park and cross the street to where the sidewalk begins. We are in front of Mrs. Kinchen's store.

But wait, is that a passenger train I hear blowing for Monitor Drive at the ice plant on East Central Avenue? We have plenty of time. No one is in a great big hurry. No one will honk their horns at us. They might even stop to talk to us or just "pass the time of day" or just see how we are feeling and see if we are going to eat at Floyd's hamburger stand in the Five-Story Building lobby or at the McClain sisters' sandwich stand on Central, next to Stone Oil Station on East Central.

Enough of that. We are waiting for the freight train to pass us at the store. It is blowing its steam whistle for the crossing at Grant Street, the busiest street in town as it is the Dixie Highway, Hwy. 129, the main route for traffic from the north to Florida.

This train is what is known as a "through freight" from Waycross to Atlanta. It is #56, still steam powered. I am quite sure it is engine #229—the tone of the whistle is unique to each engine. The engineer is either Tom McCloud or I.B. Johnson. I am not quite sure. Someone in our group thinks it is "Moon" Mullens. We will just have to see.

It is quite a hill to pull from the light plant on Hooker Street to the station where we are standing. I can see, in the distance, the curve at the light plant, so there must be about 35 or 40 box cars, a pretty good train. The deep-throated whistle sounds its warning to traffic, not an ear-splitting but a melodic note, with a column of white steam reaching for the sky, behind a cloud of black smoke that showers that end of town with cinders. I hope no good housewives have hung their white bed sheets on their clothes lines yet.

Train #56 pounds across the Johnson Street crossing, green flags fluttering on the boiler head on each side of the headlight, to tell all concerned that a second section of train #56 is behind it. The brass bell rings, a tinkling clatter. Engine #229—I was correct—drivers rolling, their white side walls shining, struggling along with its heavy cargo. The brake man is Orea Davis, the fireman is Frank Cleveland, both faithful black employees. They wave and Orea "buck dances" to the rhythm of the engine exhaust. I can't see who the engineer is, as he is on the right, or offside, of the engine, but it isn't I.B. Johnson, because he often blows the tune of "a shave and haircut" after a crossing blow. (Train #56 was a freight train routed from Waycross to Atlanta. The "drivers" were the driving wheels of the engine, which were painted white. Green flags on an engine indicated that another section was behind this train. White flags, Paul says, identified a train as an "extra" rather than a regularly scheduled one.)

As #56 labors past the depot, the train master, Fred Astin, glances at his watch, yard master J.E. "Bear" Mathis waves and engineer George Long on the switch engine sitting in the house track, #112, answers #56's whistle signal of one long and two short blasts, with two short blasts to acknowledge #56's green flags. (The "house track" was a siding for passenger trains at the depot—the "house".)

Now, who was it who said there was nothing to do in Fitzgerald, Ga.?

Well, group, shake the cinders out of your collars, but before we continue on our stroll downtown, let's let Mrs. Kinchen in her old-fashioned neighborhood store, cut us a 10-cent piece of yellow "rat" cheese off her big hoop with the wrap of cheesecloth.

She asks if we want to pay cash for the crackers and cheese or put it on our "ticket" to be settled "on pay day" or "when the eagle flies." She wipes her hands on her white apron and picks up her baby granddaughter Bonnie and bids us good day.

Let's go south on Johnson Street.

Soon we come to a nice home on the corner of Johnson and Central Avenue. This fine old house is the Ricker house. This is the first residence on West Central, unless you count the Methodist parsonage, between the Catholic and Methodist churches, which were both prominent landmarks in early Fitzgerald. (I am 18 years old and both were here as far back as I can remember.)

The Ricker house is a two-story home, now occupied by the widow Ricker. There is a definite path across her front yard, as pedestrians cut across her yard to save going around the corner as they should. We'd better not use the path as we don't want to rile her. Good day, Mrs. Ricker.

Let's stop in front of the Catholic church.

My mother told me, as a lad, that the large cement blocks were manufactured by an early Swedish immigrant, by the name of Hansen. So the stones or blocks were known as Hansen Blocks. They had the appearance of stones from medieval Europe. The building of this impressive edifice was "ol' man Dan Mahoney" straight from the Emerald Isle of Ireland, as my mother said many times. The majority of the devout members of the church were German colonists.

To name a few of the families: Father Deimel, the priest, the Kratzers, the Arbes, the Agners, the Ivemeyers, the Holtzendorfs, the Rabys, also some Drexlers, Irish as the Mahoneys, and others.

We must move on to the Lon Dickey house, which was sold to the Methodist Church as a parsonage. It is a pleasant old house, nothing grand, but shady and "homey" looking—I hate to see it being torn down to build an annex for the large Methodist Church, with the high copper cupola atop the steeple, topped by a wind vane.

I was christened in this church in 1929, but leave something to be desired as a member. I had hoped that the carillon chimes would play "The Bells of St. Mary's" as they often do. These chimes were a gift of Ms. J.L. (Maude) Perry, the very wealthy widow of a shrewd mule trader who died many years ago. Mrs. Perry is a gracious, generous lady and a friend to young people and the downtrodden.

We must decide which way to go now. Let's cross Central Avenue to the south side of the street. Maybe we should wave at ol' Raymond Harris as he tiptoes around his "Lone Star" Texaco service station. His station is popular with an emphasis on service for discriminating patrons, wiping the windshield, checking the water level, oil and battery, along with the air pressure in the balloon tires on these new model cars. He looks good in his Texaco uniform with its visored cap. Zack Bundage is his "front man." Good day, Raymond.

Let's now look back to our right, at the huge wood frame building towering behind its five huge magnolia trees. It is a shame they recently remodeled it, removing the high turrets that gave it such an elegant appearance, for it was known far and wide as the Lee-Grant Hotel. It still is the Lee-Grant, but it looks more like a huge dormitory with a wraparound porch.

We won't take time to go in and see the impressive front desk, stairway and fireplaces with their heart-pine mantels. We will speak to the proprietor, Mrs. Bowden, who with her faithful partner and bellhop, Seab Walker, is raking magnolia leaves out front. Several older natives who make their home here are sitting on the porch, probably waiting for the mail to be delivered.

Which reminds me that a few years ago, we could have seen Alvin Brown, the time-honored mailman, leaving the post office, on the corner of Central and Lee. Alvin had custom built a small, covered cart, or van perhaps. It had four wagon wheels and a "step up" at the rear. Inside, there were pigeonholes to file presented mail. This neat, compact, rolling post office was pulled by a well-trained, brown and white calico pony named Billy. Now, Billy knew the mail route as well as Alvin Brown and as Alvin went from door to door, or rather, from one mail box to the next, Billy would clop down the street, guided only by a whistle from Alvin, when to stop or start. We children would wait for the mail, give Billy a lump of sugar, jump on the step up, grab the reins and pretend we were driving a Roman chariot.

I have heard it said that there was nothing for children to do in Fitzgerald. Say that again. We are beginning to have fun on the sidewalks of Fitzgerald, aren't we?

Back to the Lee-Grant Hotel. Mrs. Bowden has a splendid dining room. Three meals a day, mid-day meal 75 cents, and surely you will leave the pretty red-headed waitress with the blue satin hair ribbon a 10-cent tip!

The civic clubs meet here, and receptions, dances—you name it—were held here. We must move on, but I want you all to know that Mrs. Bowden was a gracious Southern lady who never turned a hungry person away if he was willing to sit on the back kitchen steps and enjoy a potluck meal. She also fed the hungry teenage boys who showed up at dusk to shoot the myriad blackbirds, starlings and rice birds that rested in the magnolia trees. Many bird pies were eaten in poor families during hard times. I myself have eaten quite a few generous helpings. After all, BBs were only 5 cents a pack. Lord, I hope nothing ever happens to those glossy-leaved white blooming trees. So long, Mrs. Bowden and Sebe.

There is no doubt that you fully understand that the Lee-Grant will always hold fond memories for me and many more Fitzgerald natives, regardless of what the future holds for this splendid building and the gracious kind people around here. Oh, by the way, George Morris was the champion bird shooter.

We must press on, time waits on no one or does it? Let's step back up to the post office and move east on the south side of Central Avenue.

Now we find ourselves directly in front of the typical U.S. government building. It was standing here when I was learning how to walk with my dad, around 1930. He said I was intent on tearing down the low metal looped wire fence that ran along the sidewalk. Evidently, I was unsuccessful as it is still "looping" along there. Let me give it a kick and a shake, just for old time's sake. Yep, it is still strong.

Let's stop on the broad cement steps and glance at the signboard with the stern, craggy face of Uncle Sam pointing a long, bony finger at everyone—bold print stating, "I want you." I don't know if it was to join the Marine Corps or buy war bonds and stamps.

Inside, Miss Mina Emery, Ruth Griner and Cliff Pickens are at the windows, behind metal grids, selling stamps and money orders and receiving packages. I believe postmaster Jarrett Pryor is sitting in a separate office behind a large desk. The brass is shining and the marble floor clean. The janitress, a senior black lady, has a long gray dress on and her head is wrapped in a black cloth. She always reminds me of Whistler's Mother.

Speaking of pictures, George Washington has his eye on everyone who enters. If you happen to be late and the windows are closed, just rap on the window and call, and the window would fly open and one of the clerks in the back will give or receive your package or mail. The Adams brothers, James and Baney, are most accommodating. Hope that service will continue!

Let's leave the post office. I can't wait to see who is hanging around Harry Merritt's "filling station." Harry is a hard worker, changing oil, patching tires, or rather, inner tubes, the acid smoke of hot patches drifting into the spring air.

This is a hangout for "resting" railroad train hands. They love to line up on the sidewalk and pitch pennies to a crack in the concrete walk. The object of this serious game is to land or roll your well-worn copper penny near the designated crack. The player whose penny rests closest to the crack steps forward to proudly collect the errant pennies.

On occasion, a boy, such as I, was sent to the rear of the building to get the McCormick brothers, Albert and

Leon, who would bring the calipers out of their repair and Pontiac sales room to determine the winner, with much laughing and comments on individual marksmanship.

Alvin Knight is picking up the pennies today, he must have gathered 35. Is that John Morris, the railroad "call boy," sitting on his red Cushman scooter signing up Bozo Jordan, a locomotive engineer for a run to who knows where?

Why don't we cross over to Mrs. Gaskins' Purina Feed store and see if a shipment of biddies came in on the morning train from Atlanta? (The 1937-38 City Directory shows that Emmett R. Gaskins ran the Community Hatchery at 115 W. Central Ave. His wife was Jannie T. Gaskins.)

Some mornings in the spring of the year, once a week I think, the whole end of the express coach is stacked to the ceiling with flat cardboard cartons pierced with ventilator holes on the sides and tops, a hundred biddies to the carton. These cartons are unloaded at all the stops from Atlanta to Waycross. Cordele, Fitzgerald, Douglas and Alma got the most.

At Easter time, a shipment arrives full of biddies that are dyed all colors, just like Easter eggs. All the neighborhood kids get a dozen or two. I remember how I loved my red, yellow, blue and green biddies. I was disappointed when they molted and were black and red. Six weeks later, if you fed them well, they would be fryers, and I would tie their yellow legs with strips of cloth and put them in my bicycle basket and ride through the neighborhood shouting, "Fryers for sale, homegrown fryers for sale, fifty cents each."

How proud I would be to take my savings account book to Miss Irene Jones, a teller at the National Bank, a block down the sidewalk and see her enter three or four dollars. I thought I was well on the road to riches.

Right on the edge of the sidewalk, beside the feed

store, grows one of the largest sycamore trees in Fitzgerald. Beneath this towering tree stands a small ice house. It doesn't need a sign saying "ice for sale." Everybody knows it is there.

Every morning an ancient dump truck comes from Mr. (John Henry) Dorminy's ice plant at the east end of Central Avenue, where there are large 500-lb. blocks of clean, rock-hard ice with white "ammonia" streaks running through them. (During the freezing process, the coils carrying the refrigerant gas, left bubbly white streaks that looked like snow, Paul says.) The small wooden ice house had double walls, filled with sawdust to provide insulation. After ice was delivered to this well-shaded ice house, these large blocks would last for days.

The forms or vats the ice was molded in had distinct ridges in the metal sides. They ran vertically and horizontally, about a foot apart. These ridges left creases in the ice when the water was frozen. A man who knew what he was doing with an ice pick could chip out a 10-cent piece of ice along the grooves or creases that had been formed in the ice. Now, if you halved the newly chipped block of ice with your pick, guess what you had? A nickel piece, of course. Be it known, a kindly old gentleman by the name of Mr. Simmons could flat wield an ice pick. He must have been born with one in his hand. (Paul says a 10-cent piece of ice was about the size of a shoe box, but a little longer, while a 5-cent piece was close to the size of a honeydew melon. Frozen much harder than typical refrigerator ice today, it was long-lasting. A 10-cent piece would keep a keg of water cool for workers all day. The 50-cent piece for home ice boxes would last three to four days. While Fitzgerald Ice Company kept local citizens supplied with ice, its biggest customer was the railroad. The ice plant provided ice for the refrigerator cars. The ice house on Central was called the Ben Hill Ice Company in 1938. At that time it was run by Raymond B. Ratcliffe.)

Someone had built a small wooden deck at the base of the tree that serves as a delivery platform. Close by is a large ball of "grass" twine, strung over a sharp steel blade, positioned to cut the twine when you gave it a smart jerk. Mr. Simmons will take your nickel or dime and tie the twine around the ice, forming a handle for you to use to carry your ice home. Mr. Simmons is still strong in his arms and shoulders, but his legs and feet are "bothering" him and when he walks, he slides his feet on the sidewalk. If he had on skis and was on snow, he would be cross-country skiing. He manages to deliver ice to the nearby drug stores and filling station "drink boxes." (Paul says drink boxes at this time were insulated zinc boxes with sliding doors or doors that had to be lifted up. The customer reached into the slushy mix of ice and water and groped for a bottle. Paul describes the experience as "most refreshing.")

Bless his ole heart. Maybe before too long, everyone will have some kind of retirement plan. These old timers just have to work or depend on their children.

When I was a kid, we boys would hang around the ice house to be in the shade of the tree. There were always small chips of ice lying around, which we made ourselves welcome to. We enjoyed the "scrap ice." We ate it, threw it at each other and the bolder, braver of the group might even slip behind a non-suspecting girl and drop it down her collar and run like crazy.

The ice house is a great location in the summer to obtain gainful employment. Farmers stop for ice and, if you get there early enough, they will hire you for a day of cotton picking or peanut hoeing. Contractors are a good bet for a day job of traffic flagging or mixing mortar for a brick mason. Sort of college, in the school of hard knocks. You may even end up with two or three dollars and a great suntan.

Another never-ending attraction at the ice house are

the strings of fish, caught by local fishermen Alvin Knight, Bob Powell, Harry Merritt, C.A. Miller, R.W. "Doc" Reaves and Billy Haines. There are bream and trout caught at places like Bowen's Mill, Spring Lake (the stream that flows from Oscewicee Springs to the Ocmulgee), Coleman's pond (a lime sink where Ten-Mile Trail then ended, three miles past Land's Crossing, and down a path) Devil's Den (on the Rochelle Highway), Ballpark Lake at Lax, Knot Hole (for swimming and fishing, on Bell's Cabin Road), Lucy Lake (south of Ocilla, near Alapaha, where 129 crosses the Alapaha River), Calico Lakes (deep, clear lakes above Oscewicee), Lake Beatrice, Tiger's Leap (an oxbow on the Ocmulgee above Camp Brooklyn), Big Eddy (another oxbow just above the Jacksonville Bridge), Otter Creek, Sand Sink (in the Crystal Lake area), Burnt Fort (on the Satilla River), Trader's Hill (historic landing below Folkston on the St. Mary's), Suwannee Canal, Mobley's Bluff, Stuckey's Pond (across the Ocmulgee near Abbeville), Bussell's Mill Pond (between Mystic and Irwinville), Ruben Lake (a lime sink off the Rochelle Hwy., also called the Rocks), Rhodes Lake (above Oscewicee), Camp Brooklyn, House Creek, Sturgeon Creek, Ocean Pond (east of the game and fish complex off Hwy. 129), Brickyard and Long Lake (both on the Alapaha), Allen Worl's Smokehouse (also on the Alapaha—it was said that Allen Worl fished there instead of farming, so the river was his smokehouse), Sally Mack (below Lucy Lake, near Alapaha), Half Moon Lake (near Willacoochee), Hawk's Nest (on the Ocmulgee), close to the county landing), Williamson's Mill Pond and Boy Scout Pond (on the Tifton-Ocilla road, now Pleasure Lake) and, farther away, Orange Lake (between Ocala and Gainesville, Fla.), Lake George or maybe Cross Creek (Florida). Don't forget Billy's Lake in the Okefenokee Swamp and other far-sounding places. I'm sure there are many more good spots.

Most of these fellows end up right under that big old

sycamore tree. Man alive, if that old tree could talk, what tales it could tell.

By the way, some "city feller" stopped for ice one day and joined a group of us admiring some full-grown "trout fish" that "Duke" Massee had caught. He informed us that the splendid fish were bass not trout. Now, who has ever heard of bass?

I hope no one ever cuts that grand ol' tree down in the name of progress and rides down Central Avenue in a "streamlined" truck with four-wheel drive, balloon tires, smoked windows all rolled up tight, with air conditioning humming. Why, Mr. Simmons might be scared out of his old worn-out shoes and run off and drop his ice, string and all.

Also on the north side of Central Avenue, Colonial Stores recently built a modern "super-market"—they don't need many clerks, you just roll a buggy around the store and pick up your own items, go to the check-out stall, wait your turn in line, set your selections on the counter and a lady adds it all up. Then you claim your things and leave. It is managed by E.C. Woodard, groceries, and Mr. Arnold, meat market.

If you want my opinion of this type of store, I don't think they will ever amount to very much. No stove to warm by, no delivery boys, no brown eggs, no live chickens, no stalks of bananas, no cracker barrel, no hoops of cheese. Why Mr. Woodard has no drink box and doesn't buy empty bottles. (If you took a bottled drink out of the store, you had to pay a deposit on the bottle. You could return the empty bottle later and get your money back.) No garden seed, no bones for the dogs, no 10-cent loaves of light bread, no "bull of the woods" plug chewing tobacco with metal "tags" that all boys collect. Maybe Mr. Woodard can get a store of his own.

We must move on and look about, or I will be an old man with a long gray beard like Rip Van Winkle. I must direct your attention back down South Lee Street to the long-dilapidated building nearly behind the Lee-Grant Hotel. It is the workshop of Mr. Raines, an elderly gentleman straight out of the Wild West and the 19th century. Mr. Raines is a short, hearty man with a gray handlebar mustache. He is a master upholsterer and furniture repair man. He and his wife, with the spectacles set on her nose, are good people, so typical of the northern colonists who established Fitzgerald. Just "salt of the earth" people. Tommie Defore's auto trim shop is also located in this building. Gerald Hardin is employed here installing seat covers and such.

Now, for one of our major attractions hereabouts, directly across Lee—the Carnegie Library, a two-story brick building that has been here since I can first remember. Miss Louise Smith has retired and the delightful Pauline Ennis is librarian. Miss Ida Petrie is the operator-driver of the bookmobile that tours the county, taking books to country citizens. The upstairs is a meeting hall used by several civic clubs. The stairway up is on the alley, so as not to bother the readers downstairs. An annex on the rear is a children's section donated by Dr. Will Haile of Haile's Drug Store. I probably learned more here than I did in public schools.

Across the vacant lot on the corner of Lee and Pine we can see the White Swan Laundry, a steam-powered, full-service laundry—dry cleaning, steam pressing, banks of hot water tubs, a "battery" of women ironing white shirts, a tall smokestack belching smoke over the neighborhood. Mr. Dykes shoves split oak "bolts" into the fire box. This oak wood has been brought in by hardworking Brad Dorminy on a flatbed International truck that a train had hit and left short of a front fender, though a large spread eagle on the door was left unscratched. Brad is a fine "boy." I hope he succeeds!

Mr. Burr Stokoe, one of the first northern colonists,

established this pioneer business that works many people.

While we are in this West Pine Street area, let's not overlook Mr. Bernhardt's fruit stand. It is nothing fancy, just a shed right on the sidewalk, in front of the Holtzendorf Apartments. Mr. Bernhardt is the proprietor and is ably assisted by Miss Alice, Maggie Whitten Rabon, and his son, Victor. People walk by and pick up fruits and vegetables and pass the time of day. Everybody seems to have a few minutes to chat. I hope that never changes.

Some of the housewives now have new automobiles and gas to run them, since the war is over. They drive right up in front to make a selection. I saw one the other day with all the windows rolled up. It was a hot day, so that new car must have had "factory" air conditioning. The picture show has had air conditioning some time now. Probably won't last long, just a fad.

We have about finished this detour. Let's go back to the post office on Central (located in the building that now houses USDA offices.) and continue east. Those old train hands are still pitching pennies. The railroad extra board must be turning slowly. Is that Wilmer Stewart picking up the pennies? They will find a good home with him. (The "extra board" was the duty rotation for employees who weren't assigned to regularly scheduled trains.)

Next is Mrs. Reddock's Terminal Cafe (104 W. Central, owned by John T. Reddock in 1938). This cafe is part of a large, open-fronted building also housing the Terminal Filling Station and garage, which does grease jobs, oil changes, repairs and tires. It is operated by Ben Twitty, featuring "Woco Pep" gas. Ben also operated the Greyhound bus station before Clayton Jay built the new bus station.

The pumps have levers on the side hoses. A clear glass cylinder on top of the pump has a metal gauge prominently positioned with bold numbers on its face, from 1 to 10. When the attendant, after greeting customers and determining how many gallons of gas they desire, starts pumping the long lever on the side, the gasoline boils into the gas cylinder atop until the fluid reaches the desired digit on the gauge. Then the attendant takes the long rubber hose with the brass nozzle, places it in the auto gas tank, and the gas flows by gravity into the auto's tank.

That was okay, but the big show was that "Woco Pep" gas was red, blue and green colored to indicate the octane rating. You would just have to see that beautiful display of colored gas as it boils into that glass cylinder. Quite a show, especially at night, when the lights are on. It costs 27 cents for two gallons of regular.

We high school boys could sometimes "borrow" our father's auto, but we had to bring it home with the fuel tank indicator exactly where it was when we left the yard. We would tour the town's gas stations, which were mostly closed at night, and take the hose off the hook, hold it high and drain about a tea cup of "residue" gas into a can. We could usually get enough gas to go to Lake Beatrice if we switched off and rolled down the hill. I ask you again, nothing for young people to do in Fitzgerald?

Police Captain Milton Findley and Sgt. Tom Myers kept an eye on us—all good boys, but a little speedy at train crossings. We could usually be found at the Spotted Pig (on South Grant Street), Joe's Drive-In (on North Grant), the Silver Moon (at the corner Grant and Sultana) and Johnnie's. Kicklighter's (an all-night filling station and cafe) was nice also. But that's another tour, excuse me, group.

We don't want to miss any business or attraction, uptown or downtown. To save backtracking, let's cut behind the Grand Theatre. This alley will take us back up to the Terminal Service Station and all that pretty Woco Pep gasoline.

We are up to Elias Lovett's three-chair barber shop.

Charles Jordan's newsstand is next door, and Echol Stone has his grocery store beside the newsstand. Mr. Henderson has the meat concession—the Leggetts cut meat for him—and Cook's furniture store is on the corner at the alley.

The center square of the city is the intersection of Central Avenue and Main Street. It is a spacious brick-paved area that has witnessed many political rallies, Fourth of July celebrations, water fights, boxing matches, street dances and band concerts.

Look across to E.T. Steed's filling station (101 W. Central). Mr. Steed has branched out into several services—coal and wood yard, sand and gravel, concrete and fill dirt. He has an able crew—Luther McEwen, Curtis Dale, Spencer Scruggs, Buddy Walker, Gene and Ed Davis and Charles Steed.

Parker Higdon's wholesale grocery warehouse burned some while back, giving Mr. Steed the entire block to the railroad track.

It's a busy place, downtown. I am glad it is not Saturday, or the sidewalks would be so crowded with people that we would probably have to walk in the street.

While we are making up our minds which route to take away from here, let's identify a few people you may see on our stroll through town. These are good people, just a little different. Fitzgerald will be a little poorer when they no longer inhabit the beloved streets.

You may see Homer Waters with his "bucking" Ford, a '32 model with the rear axle set forward two feet, just enough to let the front end rear up, way up. You may see Homer at a red light with his load of passengers, usually Ted Myers, Bob Littlefield, Bowen Shepard or maybe even Roy Boles.

There is no top on the Ford, so anybody is welcome to pile in for a good time.

Homer is a big man with a great sense of humor. He

has a thick head of black hair, a plaid shirt and leather bow tie. He possesses a thunderous laugh, which he uses often. Everybody loves Homer and his piano-playing wife, Eva. You might even see the police chief, George Crawford, among his passengers.

When the light changes, Homer shoots the "blue" Woco Pep high test.   The pedal goes to the metal floorboard, the bucking Ford trembles a second and backfires even louder than those gentlemen can laugh. Instantly, the front end reaches for the sky.

Now, there is a steel plate welded to the rear bumper or, more correctly, a "skid plate."   When this strikes the brick street, fire and sparks spray up from the rear and the Ford sallies forth with the front wheels up in the air.

Wait a minute. If I am not mistaken, there is a big white English bulldog sitting next to Homer, with a black circle carefully painted around his eye. I think "Buster Brown" had one just like him in the silent movies, for which Eva Waters played "mood music" on the old off-key piano years ago.

Nothing to do in Fitzgerald? Maybe someday someone will invent "sales tax" and great projects will abound to amuse the citizens.

I hope the "bucking" Ford comes by the pearly gates and I can hear those old boys laughing. I know they will all go to heaven because they will stop to help an old lady across the street or maybe even "blind Brooks" with his white cane with the red tip on the end.

You may also see Fletcher Fussell, a mountain of a man, a hometown boy. Now 40 years old, never married, he lives with his mother on S. Lee Street. Now, Fletcher's profession is "advance man." For most carnivals, circuses, minstrel shows, even Buffalo Bill Cody and Silas Green in from New Orleans. (Silas Green had a black minstrel show, featuring black and white performers, with blues, jazz, singing and dancing.   Paul says they came to Fitzgerald in their own train car.)   Fletcher is on speaking terms with all of them and usually a pocket in his blue serge suit, which he wears summer and winter, contains free passes to the shows.   His pocket also sported an assortment of pens and pencils.

Fletcher travels statewide by rail, putting up signs for coming attractions. He is good at his job, which he has expanded to include revival meetings, especially those featuring dinner on the grounds, camp meetings and family reunions. He is rumored to be able to smell fried chicken twenty, or even more, miles away. He has witnesses to the fact that he consumed 19 pieces of chicken and half a chocolate cake. Everybody welcomes him.

His feet are very large, his shoes are referred to as rowboats and his thin blue suit is about the size of a Barnum & Bailey tent. All I am sure of is that he keeps the big cast-iron stoves in the railroad waiting rooms, both "white" and "colored," red hot on cold winter nights. He and many other "street people," including paper boys, gathered at the station at train time. (Now don't get the wrong meaning, the boys were not made out of paper. They unloaded the Atlanta Journal and Constitution newspapers off the early morning train from Atlanta for the newsstand and home delivery routes.)

I sometimes wonder what we would do without these railroad waiting rooms. You can always catch a nap on the generous benches. Chewing gum machines sell Chiclets for a penny and there is a not-too-clean rest room. Why, I even learned to read by studying the funny papers. Grown people will always help you with hard words. Water coolers located in the corner have a five-gallon glass jug of cool drinking water seated into a spigot that fills the little conical-shaped paper cups that are stacked in the wall-hung dispenser. When you open the spigot, gravity lets the water down after a gulp of air enters the bottom of the jug, resulting in a large bubble that blossoms to the water surface. Now, it is a lot more fun drinking free water at the railroad station than at home. I later learned that all containers, including buckets, were conical so they could not be taken home and used—they could not have been set down on their pointed bottoms.

That is enough railroad talk—though, after all, the railroad pays the grocery bill for a large part of Fitzgerald's families.

Now the tour must press on.

The lady wearing the broomstick skirt, white bleached "flour" sack blouse and saddle Oxford shoes thinks we should cross over Main Street to the Central Pharmacy and enjoy a cool soda. Shall we go?

A glance to the left and we see Jim Weaver scurrying around his Gulf service station. Mr. Weaver has a grease rack and a tiny shack of an office. It seems to be just large enough for him and his ticket file. He's small and his ticket file holds the tickets of his credit customers. A ticket is written for each customer, with a carbon copy for the businessman. The tickets for credit customers are kept alphabetically in a metal file box. The Fitzgerald merchants know who is good pay, slow pay and won't pay. Maybe someday there will be some kind of card used by credit customers and Jim Weaver can throw out that old file full of tickets. (The railroad paid its employees every two weeks, and when payday came, workers went around to pick up—and pay—all their "tickets." Paul says, "When times were tough, merchants had to be forbearing." Many couldn't make it without offering credit to their customers, but, conversely, many businesses failed because they couldn't collect on the credit they had extended.)

Mrs. Weaver works at the city hall, down Central and next to the fire station. Julius Bailey is city clerk there. Mrs. Weaver and Mrs. Beauchamp receive payment for water and light bills each month and woe be to those who are late paying, for the wrench man will soon perform his duties and you will find yourself in the dark and the kitchen sink will only drip.

As we mount the granite curb to the flagstone sidewalk, we find ourselves in the 100-block of East Central. This block is the heart of the business district. Let's try not to miss any business or point of interest. We may have to zigzag or backtrack to accomplish this.

I hope everyone has refreshed themselves at the soda fountain inside the Central Pharmacy. This appropriately named drug store is operated by Ed Evans and Perry Adams, only recently returned from World War II. These "docs" fill prescriptions while Mrs. Lennie Capo and her staff of soda jerks serve Coca-Colas and hamburgers to the public—butchers, bakers, candlestick makers, and loads of kids when school lets out. Lots of fun, but let's press on.

Let's stroll east down the center parks of spacious Central Avenue so I can point out the thriving businesses on either side of the avenue. Perhaps you wouldn't walk down the parks, but Fitzgerald is a friendly town that would welcome a group of sightseers and believe me, there are some sights to see.

There is no nicer cop on the beat than Shorty Grantham. He would probably just join us. So let's go.

We have already spoken to Jim Weaver juning around his Gulf station on the corner. On the left are vacant lots, covered with kudzu vines. Rumor is that the telephone company is planning to build a new exchange there.

Let's now look to the right, to the glass front of the Home Furniture Co., owned by Mr. Jimmy Paulk, prominent merchant, undertaker and mayor of the town. (The founder was Mr. Littlefield, deceased.) Mr. Paulk's sons assist him in the business, Etheridge "Flip" and Donnie, but Ellis is going to coach football and teach school and Mickey is away at school. Fine boys! Susie Braswell works here and Jake Brewer repairs furniture upstairs. He also assembles furniture that arrives unassembled.

While we're at Home Furniture Co., we should take a look at Elmer Archer's barber shop. Elmer is a second generation barber. His father, Burt Archer, was one of the town's first barbers. He must have been sitting on a stump sharpening his shears, waiting on the first northern colonist to arrive in Fitzgerald.

Perhaps this would be a good time to mention a few other barbers who practice their profession at various locations uptown—"Coot" Norris, the Hilton boys, Bill Branam, Red Raines, the Lovett Brothers, "Big Boy" Hall, Charlie Coleman, Doc Deese, Walter Owens. All these are good men, hard working and honest. They could qualify for an honorary degree in psychology. They without a doubt hear more sad stories, counsel more unhappy marriages, save more shootings, influence more elections, pour out more liquor and tell more funny stories than anybody. They also know more important dates and facts—like when fishing season comes in, where the fish are biting, which engineer on the railroad brought the passenger train in on time, all the ball scores, where the best food in town is being served, who is having a cane grinding and who has run off with whom.

As we move on, the newspaper office comes into view, Pryor Brothers Printing—the Fitzgerald Herald (111 E. Central). S.G. Pryor is the editor. Irene Royal works in the front. This is a busy place, setting type, presses rolling. The paper comes out Tuesday and Friday.

The local newspaper doesn't need any reporters. S.G. Pryor can just tour the barber shops, and while he gets a shave, haircut and his shoes shined, he also gets the "lowdown" on the weekend's activities. He only publishes the paper for the record. Then you can bundle them up and sell them to the fish markets to wrap fish in to take home. Thus the street name of the local publication is the "mullet wrapper."

Langley's Shoe Shop takes us to the alley. The Langleys were running this shoe repair business when I was a boy. They will mend your shoes and put steel taps on the heels and toes. You can drop off your shoes to be shined by the shoeshine boy. The place smells of Shinola polish and neat's-foot oil and sheets of leather the "boys" shape into soles. A heavy duty sewing machine stitches the soles to the original uppers. A row of graded buffers smooths the raw edges of the new soles and, with new laces, the shoes look like new. Until recently shoes were rationed, so business is brisk. I think there is a new word for this operation—"recycling."

Could I point out that all of these brick buildings were laid up by Italian and Irish brick-laying gangs who lived in camps and boarding houses around town in the 1890s? So my Yankee mother told me. The stairs lead upstairs to long halls that give entry to dwelling apartments and storage rooms.

These apartments were occupied by the owners and proprietors of the businesses until they prospered and built homes down the street. Now mostly renters and street people live up there. These people come down in the evening to cool off and chat with passers by. They really don't even need an automobile.

To our left on Central Avenue, extending to Grant Street, is the United Wholesale Co. This is the wholesale dry goods warehouse operated by our Jewish citizens. Many retail stores here and around south Georgia are supplied from here. (Paul says that Phillip Halperin and several other Jewish merchants formed the wholesale company. They purchased from wholesalers in New York. Paul can recall seeing a boxcar load of shoes being delivered to the warehouse. Bulk shipments would be broken down into packaged goods for the different stores supplied by United Wholesale Co., each receiving the type of items that sold well in its community). I hear that the Segraves brothers, Owen and Marion, want the building for a furniture store.

Many changes are happening in this post-war era. We stand on the threshold of new and different business methods. Change is in the wind.

I have hopped over to Mr. Harry Vinson's Chrysler auto sales show room and repair garage (Vinson Motor Company, 116 E. Central). Mr. Vinson is one of Fitzgerald's first auto salesmen. He is crippled and walks with a stout walking stick. His voice makes up for his bad legs, as he can talk to you a block away. He terms himself as the "whole cheese," not just a slice. Let's move on before he or his son, Billy, sell us a little four-door Plymouth with the four-mast sailing ship for a hood ornament.

Vinson Auto and the United Wholesale have taken us to the crossing of Grant Street and Central Avenue. We must now look to our right, or the south side of Central Avenue, to complete the 100-block. The alley separates Langley Shoes from the Southeastern Telephone Exchange and front office. Louise Mathis will be glad to receive your payment for your phone bill. Mr. Tuttle, or "Tut," is engineer and several operators are on duty to ask "number, please." A busy place. Telephones are proliferating since the war is over. This small building is outgrown and is soon to be replaced.

I don't feel that I have fully covered this subject, as I would hate for some poor uninformed, innocent tour member to leave this spot of ground in the park—with the towering oak and elm trees, three jelly palms at each end, paths worn ankle deep by the many pedestrians or jaywalkers who cut across this park to trade with merchants or just shake hands with their friends or neighbors (several of the more prosperous have telephones and have come to pay their "phone bills")—without seeing everything.

And look, there goes Wade Malcolm, who is certainly another "town character." Wade is selling Venetian blinds, now, as you can tell if you look at his truck. The sign on the side reads: "This truck is being driven by a blinds man."

Going back to the barber shops, with their red and white, candy-striped poles displayed out front—they open at eight o'clock and close when the last customer has been served, usually around eight or nine o'clock on week nights and in the wee morning hours on Saturday night.

Let it be said here and now, there isn't much running hot water in Fitzgerald, or hereabouts, unless you build a fire in the "jacket" heater and wait an hour for it to heat. There was always hot water at the barber shops as the heaters only cooled on Sunday, a day of rest (except on the railroad). Lots of men took hot baths late Saturday night, sometimes referred to as "bath night," followed by a shave and a haircut and a "high-smelling" hair tonic, liberally applied to plaster the new haircut down. The hair tonic could still be smelled at church next morning as these tired men peacefully slept in the pews.

We boys went to the barbershop, too, from the time a board had to be placed across the arm rest so our little butts were up high enough for the barber to reach our heads and perform another "masterpiece." Sometimes an adoring mother would accompany her little darling for his first haircut, drying his tears and saving his long tresses for the scrapbook. My own mother cried when the price came to 50 cents.

We get "flat tops" and "GI" and "sugar bowl" cuts, price 35¢. After each cut, the barber lights fire to a special wooden stick and singes the "wild hairs." The smoke and odor terrify kids.

In Fitzgerald's streets, we boys sold boiled peanuts,

read the funny papers (comics) and furthered our education and vocabulary greatly, with things we would probably have never learned at dear old Fitz High. (Paul says he was a street peddler as a child and, in addition to peanuts, sold his mother's homemade divinity, with half a pecan on each piece, for 10 cents each. He had to buy the Karo syrup and pick out the nuts. He remembers that the ladies at the post office were especially fond of these.)

I could go on and on, but I see my friends are ready to continue our tour. Forgive me! We hope to get around to Wiley Floyd's hamburger stand in the Five Story Building for lunch.

Just east of the telephone office is a flight of stairs going up to the second story of the National Bank building. Let's take the stairs and go up to the offices located on both sides of a dreary, dark hall. The floorboards are old and creak and groan as we venture down the hall.

Most of the offices are vacant. I will list a few tenants who are here or have been here. The bank owns this obsolete building that now has mostly county and state offices, for which the Ben Hill County Commissioners must furnish space. The rent is cheap and the bank appreciates the income, so who wants to offend the bank? Maybe it will someday have air conditioning. It now has electric fans. Or maybe it will be torn down and become a parking lot, which is badly needed.

Present or past tenants include the state highway department, Ralph Sweat, director, and Jim Collier (or Henry Harden), county agent, and the home demonstration agent. Great people. Across the hall is B.L. "Red" Walters, soil conservation technician, and Paul Dunn, part-time aid. That Dunn scamp is trying to work for the railroad and help Red—he can't last long.

The ASC farm commodity group has headquarters here, with Ralph Pope as head man and Leo Roberts as area supervisor. Miriam Sanderford, Karen Swanson and

Carolyn Walker are clerks. Love them all.

Let's say goodbye to these hard-working folks and regroup on the sidewalk, these shoes are killing me. I see several of you are toting yours.

Moving east on Central Avenue, on the right-hand side of the double street, I doubt if we will see John Y. Brown or his sister Alma McLendon, hard at work trying to beautify the female population. Men are not allowed or encouraged to visit their shop. I could be wrong, but I think the name is Beauty Bob. (The Beauty Bob had an earlier location on S. Main Street.)

Now, there is no gossiping or local news events ever spoken of in these shops. I might be wrong again, you decide. I did see a stack of well-worn magazines in the garbage box entitled True Love, Romance Today, Woman's Home Companion, Movie News and Hollywood Confessions.

I did one day glance in the open door and these women had their heads under a hood, called a dryer. Others had electric wires from the ceiling attached to their hair. Can you believe this? All in the name of beauty. A lot of cigarette smoke was leaving there also.

Maybe I will know more about the next business, the F.R. Justice Co., Real Estate, Insurance. Mr. Frank came to Fitzgerald with the colony and is the "prestige gentleman" in this line of endeavor. The company logo is a picture of the earth with the words "We sell the earth and rent the town" and they well near live up to that motto. As a lad, I saw Mr. Justice and his tiny wife in this office, along with their sons, Arthur and Lawrence Earl Justice. They are very important people in Fitzgerald. Honesty and professionalism are personified here.

Let's look around and see what I have overlooked. Sure enough, here comes Malcolm Reese, the loan officer for the Federal Savings and Loan office located in this block of East Central. Since the war is over and peace is here, the government has encouraged home building by providing money, or loans, at affordable rates so people in the street can afford nice homes. Good day, Malcolm. We may be seeing you soon. Lonnie V. Owens is his secretary and treasurer.

The Clip and Curl Beauty Shop is last before we get to the bank. I hate to hear that plans are to tear this little building down, to make a driveway for the drive-through window the bank is proposing. People can do their negotiations sitting right under the steering wheel of their car, which the bank is probably financing for them. They won't get to see everybody and see the smiling faces of the bank employees. Probably won't many people ever use it, but that's progress, I reckon—tear it down.

Now, Mrs. Alice Bowles, one of Fitzgerald's most beloved ladies, operates the little—maybe I should be "uptown" and refer to it as a beauty salon. She is the widow of one of the first electricians Fitzgerald was honored to have, Yancey Bowles.

When Miss Alice worked in Abe Kurger's department store as a sales lady, she wore a ribbon around her neck, a pair of four-inch scissors attached, for clipping cloth before she tore it into lengths. She could measure cloth off a bolt of yard goods, stripping it off, passing it from her nose to her fingers a yard at the time. She could do it before she could remove her tape measure from her waist. I don't reckon she ever made a mistake, cause if all the cloth she had dispensed was strung out, it probably would reach to the moon and halfway back.

After the war, ladies began buying ready-made dresses and clothing. So Miss Alice started a new career. Lots of ladies patronized her, including my mom, Tessie. There probably won't ever be an equal to her.

She was a little plain spoken. I hope I never forget her at church on Sundays, her shock of white hair, bobbed in the back, her generous, corseted figure, high-heeled shoes, colorful beaded pocketbook and a big, broad-brimmed "flop" hat set at a cocky angle, fanning the gnats away with a colorful Japanese fold-up fan. That preacher, Ed Fain, I think had better have a good sermon, cause she is on the pulpit committee. Hate to see old Ed sent to Ambrose.

I can't leave this location without telling you good people about one of the early tenants of this little nook. As you understand, Fitzgerald has a unique history as an "instant town"—just add all sorts of people and fellow travelers, anybody that can see lightning or hear thunder, and shake well. It wasn't just Yanks and Rebels. People were trying to rebuild a war-torn, bitter nation after the Civil War. I wasn't born yet, but my mom was a Yank and my dad a "pore cracker" lad dropped by fate in a roaring boomtown, because he could telegraph using the Morse Code. So I heard many yarns about Shacktown as it was first known.

More credit should have gone to the stalwart senior women who guided this unruly multitude to the law-abiding, God-fearing town it has become (with a few exceptions). So I must tell you good folks about "Ma" Forbes, a mere slip of a tired-looking woman, long dead, rest her weary bones. She had a thriving sewing room at this location. (Mrs. Mattie Forbes. Her shop was located at 127 E. Central in 1938.) I was so young, that all I am sure of is that from dawn to dark, Ma was bent over a big Singer sewing machine that was roaring away as she guided material to a needle that was just a blur. She seldom looked up. Ladies would buy a pattern—Butterick, Simplicity, Vogue, McCall's—select materials, buttons, thread, etc., and take them to Ma Forbes.

What impressed me were the beautiful flowers, pot plants, African violets, ferns and gloxinias blooming in profusion in the dead of winter. The large glass windows let in just the right light and the wood stove, with the hot water kettle whistling as wisps of steam came out, kept the humidity very high. In fact, the windows were usually fogged.

Ma had raised a good crowd of boys and girls with a one-legged husband who could no longer work. She was plain spoken, almost abrupt. My mom told me that Ma Forbes was highly respected and when she spoke, people listened. I don't know what had happened, but on several occasions during Fitzgerald's lawless beginnings, and there were some, Ma's word was the law, judge and jury.

She called my dad in one day and told me to wait on this very sidewalk we're standing on today. She went back to her sewing machine and began to stitch again. She admonished my dad to correct himself and straighten up, so my mom later told me. He had his hat in his hand as she talked. He was "born again" then and changed his ways. I understand this happened many times in the twenties and thirties. I don't know why there isn't a statue of her in the park, but after all, we are just talking about respect. One day she was gone. Just gone.

Now let's move back to the last business establishment on this block, the National Bank of Fitzgerald, a landmark structure in downtown Fitzgerald. The builders were masters of their trades around the turn of the century, I guess. Let's go inside, although we only have a little pocket change on us.

Mr. C. A. "Charlie" Newcomer is president, a second generation Northern colonist. His very appearance is that of a banker, and he has skillfully guided this bank through many financial crises. Mark Mathis is cashier and loan manager. He knows everyone and their ability to repay loans. Mark is known for his Christian ethics and his ability to put his foot down and say "no" without making an enemy.

Miss Irene Jones is a cashier, a career girl. I can't imagine her ever making a mistake counting stacks of money. C.T. Owens comes from a good Southern family. He is well liked as he sits behind another teller window. His sister, Mrs. Eleanor McLendon, is probably the prestige history teacher at Fitz-High. She also coaches the debate team. Many men and women revere her name. She even taught me some things. She should have taught me spelling.

James Mahoney, son of a colonist, an Irish immigrant, is at another window, a fine-looking lad, come up as a clerk in the Great Atlantic and Pacific Tea Co. (A&P Store), he knows how to greet people. Some of the ladies think he is good looking. Ah, a little Irish charm never hurt anything. Eltheda Roberts is very efficient as Mr. Newcomer's secretary.

I loved them all when I came in here to deposit 25¢ in my bank savings account. As a child I had a little bank book in my own name, and how proud I was to see it slowly grow.

The last window is occupied by Mrs. Holland Davis, a young woman who has been hired recently.

Upstairs is the bookkeeping department. You never see much of them. I think Lillian Evans is the spark plug up there. The board of directors consists of the top businessmen in Fitzgerald. Mr. J.H. Dorminy Jr. and Mr. Jim Parrott are important members, along with Col. J.C. "Carlisle" McDonald, attorney. I think we can sleep well knowing that what little money we have is in good hands.

I might add that some new banks are opening on the horizon. Things are restless here on the business front now that the war is over and the men are home from far lands with strange-sounding names. They have seen a lot. The "old guard" better take note. Change is in the wind. Every time I come uptown, something is being changed—new businesses, new buildings, more traffic and people. I am becoming a stranger in my own town.

It was once said, "Only fools and dead men don't

change their minds." So who knows—the future is not ours to see. I just hope I will be around.

Now let's all wait for a green light to cross Grant Street, which is also Hwy. 129, the old and famous "Dixie Highway," the main line to fabulous Florida. I have seen some come through in Cadillacs only to go back North with a pack on their back or riding the rails on a freight train.

We have just stepped on the curb of the 200-block of East Central Avenue. The first building caught our attention before we mounted the curb. It is the Dr. Pepper bottling plant. Curtis Green is manager, Pat Stafford Sr., operations superintendent, and Leonard Walker, distributor. The products are Dr. Pepper, Buffalo Rock, 7-Up, Orange Crush and all flavors of fruit sodas. (Buffalo Rock was a ginger ale, packaged in a special brown bottle that flared out at top and bottom and narrowed in the middle.)

The thing of interest to boys and girls is the long conveyor belt, or track that circles the large room and carries the freshly bottled drinks—bottles, mind you, not cans—single file to the workers who grab them, two at a time, to place them in the wooden crates, then take them to the delivery truck.

I would not have completed this description if I didn't mention the sweet little woman who sits in a high chair and visually inspects each bottle as it passes by for unseated caps or cracked glass. (We boys also mentioned roaches and flies.) At the Coca-Cola plant down on Grant Street, Mrs. George Ellis performs this task.

All this operation is inside, right along the sidewalk. All that keeps a person from reaching over and getting a bottle is a huge, plate glass window.

On the days the fruit sodas are bottled, there are drinks of every color: red (cherry), yellow (pineapple), green (lime), orange, etc.

It is quite a popular place on hot afternoons. The staff is friendly and all you have to do to get a drink is to walk in and smile. They will say, "One on the house." You stay until you've finished drinking then put your bottle in the empty rack.

This is a great time to be a young person in a small town. Everyone knows each other. You are expected to behave and be ladies and gentlemen. I would hate to think what my mom and especially my dad would have done to me if Curtis Green had told them that I "cut the fool" or "acted the hog" at the bottling plant.

Maybe this is a good time to express my impression of conduct in our fair city. I think Sheriff Frank Ellis summed it up with a simple statement: "If it weren't for 12 people in Ben Hill County, I would be out of a job." Enough said.

If a merchant isn't cheerful, honest, tolerant and clean, he will soon be out of business. If you are immoral very long, you will be presented with a train or Greyhound bus ticket to Timbuktu.

There are things that go on, but they aren't flaunted. And heaven help anyone who molests a child or an old person. Your civil rights will no longer exist.

There was a time in Fitzgerald when there was little or no law enforcement, only vigilantes or "night riders." But my grandmother told me that the passenger train stopped at the depot one day and a small man stepped from the coach. A group of prominent men encircled him and when they had dispersed, Fitzgerald had a new constable, Officer Smitts.

He spoke little—English or German. He just kept oiling a Colt six-shooter, throwing bottle crowns in the air, drawing his trusty gun, shooting and sending the crowns whirling into the next county. He rode a bicycle, one with a high-spoked wheel in front and a small wheel behind.

There were 22 open barrooms and bordellos on E.

Pine Street at the time the little constable arrived. He had no friends, no family. No one knew who paid him or where he came from. He ate his lunch sitting on the curb, back to a brick wall. He put on quite an exhibition shooting and lived in a rooming house on the wrong side of the tracks.

When he arrived, no lady turned the corner at the Five-Story Building and walked alone down E. Pine Street. But within a month, children were playing on the street, ladies were tying their horses to hitching posts and there were lots of vacant storefronts on E. Pine. A functioning police force was again visible.

The little constable caught the night train, the "Rattler" as it was referred to, and he was never seen or heard from again. And you know, he never was known to shoot anyone. What was it—have gun, will travel?

Maybe we should take up a collection and get a statue of a small man with a big gun and a bright, five-pointed star on his leather vest. Let's put it right next to Ma Forbes' statue, right out there in the Central Avenue park.

Upstairs, above the Dr. Pepper bottling plant, is the Perfect Pants sewing plant. Let's take time to go around the corner to the S. Grant Street stairs and freight elevator that lead up to this bustling business.

Well, bless Pat, there's Glenn Wallace, a big fine young man, strong as two men like me. He is a drayman, hauling cardboard cartons that look like they have been used before from the elevator of Perfect Pants to the railroad depot for shipment to who knows where, maybe to New York City or even Paris, France.

Let's struggle up these steep well-worn wooden stairs before Glenn puts us to helping him heave those cartons of pants into his pre-war red van. Maybe it will make it to the freight depot.   If it won't, Glenn could probably push it there.

As we gain the landing, we wonder if this little "office" or rather "cubbyhole" could be the nerve center of such a thriving business. I see a young woman. Must be Hurley Merritt—it is, sitting behind a stack of paperwork. Hurley is always cheerful and smiling. Why, she hasn't room, as they remark, to cuss a cat in this so-called office, which she shares with her boss and another worker.

We are lucky. Here comes Dick Kaminsky, owner-operator of this booming sewing factory. Now Dick is transplanted to Fitzgerald from the sewing district of New York City. He himself is a native of Brooklyn. That's not hard to believe as he has a very Brooklyn brogue. He has to shout to be heard above the rows of sewing machines that are roaring away, stitching the stacks of cut out pants. These local girls and women are working on a production schedule and their fingers are flying.

Now Dick has some new equipment to mass produce pants. He and his New York partner have introduced an electric cutter that zips through stacks of cloth, producing dozens of pants parts, like they were hot butter. Dick was fortunate to get the Luke brothers, Bill and Russell, to work for him. They operate these cutters. They can cut enough pants to keep this large group of women at work. Bill is the plant superintendent. He designs the pants and makes the patterns.

We won't keep Dick long. He has his tape measure in his hand and a cigar clenched in his teeth. We all agree that he needs a much larger factory. I feel he is going to put Fitzgerald on the map and put some much needed cash in these dedicated workers' pockets. Dick also has three sons, Tavin, Larry and Penny, who are being raised in the garment industry.

Let's backtrack to East Central Avenue, past the Dr. Pepper plant to the next business: Tomlin's Radio & Television Repair and Sales. Tommy, as he's known, learned his trade in the service. His wife helps him in sales and bookkeeping. There is a local "kid," Don Norris, apprenticed to Tommy. Looks like they have a rosy future, as everyone wants a television, and he has a long-standing trademark, Zenith. (Paul says that TVs were more expensive then than they are now, like air conditioners, and attention was given to providing them with furniture-grade cabinets.)

Mrs. Tomlin has specimen pot plants in the window and chairs to sit on, just to chat a spell, but we have already chatted too much.

We must move on to Johnnie Garrison's grocery store. This could well be one of our favorite stops. Johnnie is a hard-working likable young man. Slender, straight brown hair, "roached" (slickly combed back), an apron, white, with a bib and strings tied around his waist. He has a smile of welcome.

He is known far and wide as a grocery merchant. His store is not one of the modern "super" markets that are springing up all over. His store is an old-fashioned one with a long wooden counter holding a well-used cash register and a large roll of wrapping paper that can be torn off at the desired length as a metal cutter rides the portion pulled off. There is also a stack of brown paper bags, or maybe I should say several stacks, of graduating sizes, and a roll of twine and gummed tape.

While we have our minds on packaging, have you ever seen a live chicken—hen, pullet or fryer—packaged "to go"? First, you securely tie the bird's yellow feet together with a piece of cord, next you select a brown paper bag, the correct size to accommodate the critter's body, tear a corner off the bottom of the sack, then carefully ease the chicken's carcass into the open sack until, with some manipulation, the head emerges through the hole you have made. Then you quickly tie the mouth of the bag with a "tag" of the string that you have used to bind the feet. The bird can't flap his wings, walk or otherwise resist. The customer grabs the feet and proceeds down the sidewalk, leaving a lot of cackling chickens still in crates, a cloud of dust and a few feathers cartwheeling to the rough wooden floor of the store.

These old-fashioned stores are still doing a good business and several are still in downtown Fitzgerald. I can see that the bell has tolled for this type of marketing, probably with the demise of the present adult generation. So, I may dwell on this typical store, for the record.

Farmers are still coming to town on Saturday afternoons to trade for their staple groceries, about half of them have come in wagons drawn by mules and two or three by big, lumbering, spotted oxen, slavering at the mouth as they chew their cud. Oxen don't have to have bits in their mouths. They had a bridle, and the lines were attached to it. (Oxen, castrated bulls, were guided primarily by voice commands. Paul says they were well trained and raised for the work of hauling things. They were used for pulling logs, too, but by 1946 there were not very many around. Paul describes the oxen as "very steady, very slow" and says they would never run away. Mules continued in service as draft animals longer than oxen, Paul says, because tobacco farmers needed them. They couldn't get a tractor between the rows in a tobacco field to do the cultivating, but a mule could pull a plow through.)

Better look quick, because when these are gone an era will close. There is no problem with DUI as the patient animals know the way home and to their lot where their hay awaits them. The driver may be passed out and his wife bedding down the young'uns in the wagon bed—the mules are the designated drivers. And these drivers won't have their pictures in the local newspaper next week and they won't ever have to pick up trash along the road. And the good woman will just say, "He worked hard this week and is tired. Let him sleep." He will be sitting in church

Sunday morning. Unless he raised hell or got into a fight, then he is in the jailhouse now.

Let's turn our attention back to Johnnie's store. Could I say that it is a rural store in an urban setting? Let me touch on an item that moves fast here—Octagon soap. All the wives and children save the coupons on the wrapper to trade in on many useful items. Other products include Arm & Hammer baking soda, Red Devil lye, Red Diamond kitchen matches, Avery Island salt, Quaker oatmeal, Post Toasties, "kit fish"—salt mackerel in a wooden bucket (Paul says the salt mackerel was popular with country people as a breakfast food. The fish had to be washed and soaked overnight, to leach out some of the salt with which it was preserved. The fish was not fried, he says.), Nabisco cookies, Swan hand soap, Pet canned milk, Dixie Crystals sugar, Karo syrup, Dole pineapple, Lipton and Tetley tea, Duz soap powder, hoop cheese, Maine sardines, soda crackers, five gallons of whole dill pickles sold by the pickle, hog lard, by the pound carton or by the five-gallon metal can, salt pork, sow belly or streak-of-lean, also known as "sawmill chicken," sliced as ordered, Aladdin lamp mantels, rolls of lamp wick, lamp chimneys and kerosene lamps themselves, wash tubs, buckets, scrub boards, bleach, Argo corn starch, clothes pins, dried raisins, prunes, peaches and apricots, candied fruit, pineapple, cherries and citron—mostly these were sold from Thanksgiving through Christmas (for making fruitcakes).

A hot line of goods is vegetable seeds and plants—cabbage, collard, onion and tomato plants. Everyone has a spring and fall garden.

A cabinet of shelves is well stocked with spices and seasonings: pepper, nutmeg, tall bottles of vanilla flavoring, cloves, allspice, cinnamon and ginger. Men bought cloves to suck on to kill alcohol breath.

Along the walls are stacks of livestock feed in cloth sacks, in bold colors and prints. When emptied, these sacks were cut open, washed and bleached (if white), sunned on clothes lines and fences and carefully cut by loving mothers into clothes for the family, from underwear to blouses. Nothing was thrown away.

Feed was formulated for chickens: scratch feed, biddy starter and laying mash, sold to order from a pound to a ton. (Scratch feed was the all-purpose feed, scattered by hand for the chickens. Biddy starter and laying mash provided the extra protein that a laying hen or newly hatched biddy needed.) There was also horse and mule feed, dairy feed for milk cows, along with cotton seed meal and hulls for Ol' Bossy, cause those babies needed milk and butter.

How good a batch of biscuits is, cooked in a wood stove oven with a pound of cow butter churned and molded with the print of a four-leaf clover on top. Pass the syrup, will you?

Tobacco products were well represented. Most men smoked whatever they could get their hands on, beg, borrow or steal. In fact, a male was not considered grown until he wore long pants, shaved once a week, at least, and chewed, smoked, or dipped snuff without getting sick or having tears running down his face.

Johnnie had Prince Albert, in the can, Bugler and Bull Durham in the sack, "leaves" or papers to roll your own, "tailor made," packages of Camels, Lucky Strikes, Kools, Raleighs (they also had coupons), Phillip Morris and Avon. A few brave souls smoke a very strong cigarette named Picayune or Home Run. Hold on!

Older women loved their snuff—Buttercup, Red Rose, Bruton and Strawberry. I often hear men call cigarettes "coffin tacks," and I wonder why.

Let's not overlook the flour, meal and grits department. Flour is marketed in cloth sacks, similar to muslin. The material is valuable to the housewife, who uses it to strain raw milk, dry dishes and make underclothes and drawstring blouses with puffed sleeves.

Grits and corn meal are staples in the kitchen. Both white and yellow varieties of corn meal are used. Popular brands are Arnett's and Dixie Lily, in 2 1/2-, 5-and 10-lb. bags. Flour is very important, used in cakes, pastries, dumplings, biscuits and hoecake, mixed in a handmade magnolia wood dough bowl. The kitchen was unequipped without one, along with a rolling pin that, when placed properly against the head of a man, would raise a knot the size of a hen egg and settle most disagreements.

Popular flour brands were Twinida, Napa's Best, Pillsbury, Shawnee Maid and White Lily. All brands are plain or self rising, your choice.

(Paul says that there were three mills grinding corn for grits or cornmeal in the 1940s—at Bowen's Mill and Lake Beatrice and on W. Roanoke Drive, across from where the old radio station is, Brooks Davis operated a gas-driven mill. The gas-powered mill was faster than the water-turned one, but Paul says the taste of meal from the water-powered mills, which ground more slowly and didn't transfer as much heat to the meal, was preferred. There was plenty of corn grown in the community, and folks had cornbread during the week, Paul says. Flour had to be purchased and that made biscuits a Sunday dish only for some.)

Several older men and young boys are employed mainly on weekends to wait on customers and carry out groceries to trucks and wagons parked on vacant lots and alleys behind stores. I can see men with a 25-lb. sack of flour with a piece of wrapping paper around the middle, tied with a piece of string, over one shoulder and a sound asleep young'un on the other, headed for the wagon at about 10 p.m. on a Saturday night—with a brood of children being herded along by Mama, going home, humble as it might be.

(The piece of wrapping paper around the flour sack

was there to indicate that it had been purchased, Paul says.)

There were schools about the county that had lunch rooms—Lynwood, Tapley, Emory, Roanoke, Ashton and Cotton Mill bought groceries by the week. Johnny would charge these to the county school board. He was glad to have such an account.

I see two lunch room workers I am acquainted with today, loading supplies into a stripped down Model A Ford truck named Robin, manned by Willa Ree Tucker and Sudie Player, hardworking lunch room helpers and volunteer mothers at New Tapley School, up the Ten Mile Trail, deep in Irwin County (but that doesn't matter, as people from everywhere love to trade in Fitzgerald).

In the rear of the store is a large coal stove with a long stove pipe to give heat in winter and a huge electric exhaust fan to keep the store cool in summer. Several empty nail kegs and cane-bottomed chairs circle about, well attended by retirees and resting farmers, who probably had their crops "laid by." (Farmers were "laid by" when their crops had grown too big for them to be able to get the mule and plow into the field to cultivate. The corn had tassled out, the peanuts covered the rows, generally by the second week in June. When the farmer had done the last side dressing, the last cultivating, from that time on the success of his crop was in God's hands, Paul says, and the crops were "laid by.")

They entertain themselves with political news, crop conditions, war rumors, rainfall and frost threats. (The Cold War slowly developed in the years following the close of World War II, as central Europe was partitioned between East and West. It was in 1946 that Sir Winston Churchill warned of an "iron curtain" falling across Europe.)

But by and large, it is the ongoing checker game, played on a homemade checker board, that is the attraction. The checkers, or "men," are metal bottle tops or crowns which, are plentiful at the "cold drink" box.

I see Jessie Coan, Lamar Smith, O.M. Thomas, Sherman Arthur, Garland Cowan, Mr. J.H. Stuart, O.C. Tyre, Grover Forsythe, George Talbot and O.C. Langford. These regulars are apt to be discussing last Saturday's fox "race" or hunt, noting which hound dog was in the lead—Pepper, Francie, Bugle Ann, Big Boy or Belle, maybe even Ol' Street, a cur that was always around town and often got loaded with the foxhounds.

(Don't imagine elegant British foxhounds and mounted hunters dressed in their "hunting pink." South Georgia fox hunts were just a bit different, Paul says. There were no horses involved and the fox was the least important part of the venture. The hunting men, mostly retired citizens, gathered at the railroad depot around 3:30 a.m. on Saturdays. They would load up some dogs, including any strays around that were interested—the dogs would come running when they blew the horn—and go out into the county. "The dogs did all the hunting," Paul says. "The men stood by the fire and talked. It was a social gathering." There was competition among the men about which dog would be nearest the fox when it was "treed." "Fascinating stories were told around the fire," Paul says. As a boy, he was often one of the party—he could climb a tree and knock the fox down, he says. The men involved knew the woods and fields thoroughly. And sometimes, he says, they let the fox go, so they could have another hunt the next Saturday. Landowners considered the fox hunts a service, as the foxes preyed on chickens and small livestock. Paul says he made a lot of friends on these hunts. "They were good men.")

There should be a leash law, but what would men do for hunting dogs? And garbage disposal? Someone asked the sheriff—Virgil Wells, I think—why he didn't shoot some of these stray dogs. He retorted, "One of these dogs may belong to some kid that someday may be able to vote."

Mary Coleman's "Mary's Cafe," also in the 200-block of E. Central, is our next stop. She and her workers and father Silas are preparing for the mid-day crowd that flocks here to enjoy her Southern "home" cooking.

Many of Fitzgerald's delightful senior citizens appear at noon. I believe I see Mrs. George P. Morris arriving. She is one of my best friends. She is a relative of Mr. W. R. Bowen, one of the prominent Southern land owners who were well established around-about here when the Northern colonists arrived in 1894-96. She is very knowledgeable of Fitzgerald's early history. I love Mrs. Morris. We got acquainted when I was but a lad. Mrs. Morris goes back to settlement days.

Mr. W. R. Bowen, instrumental in the establishment of Fitzgerald, was a wise and capable Southern land owner and businessman.

Brooks' Auto Supply is next. Automobiles are big business since the war and several new stores in town have a large supply of auto parts, so vital to keeping this fleet operating.

A vacant filling station takes us to the alley.

I realize, as I stand at this corner, that it's time for the afternoon passenger train from Atlanta, #101, to arrive at the depot. Dewey Butler is the regular engineer, who will be relieved, as will his black fireman, Sam Thomas.

The arrival of today's train brings back vivid memories of a bygone day that will never be forgotten in Fitzgerald, with its love for the railroad and a popular new president.

I was but a small child in the mid 1930s when my father, Ted Dunn, rushed in at noon to announce that President Franklin Delano Roosevelt would be the guest of the president of the AB&C Railroad, Col. Bugg, on his private office car, #101. My father was excited about the once-in-a-lifetime visit of a real live president to the Colony City. The president would appear on the rear vestibule of the private car and make a short speech to the crowd that would gather.

It would take 15-20 minutes for the steam locomotives to be changed out, and the train crew that had brought the train from Atlanta, 205 miles to the north, to be relieved.   During this time, the city officials would welcome the president and the president would make his address. My father was on the welcome committee, as he was the railroad agent, along with Newton Mathis, ticket agent.

My father had gathered two dozen red roses from his rose garden and instructed my mother to dress me for the occasion, as he wanted me to present the flowers to President Roosevelt. I was old enough to appreciate the magnitude of this visit, as this president's name had become a household word.

My mother, Tessie, groomed both me and the roses. At train time, my father picked us up and we went to the passenger depot, where this tour began this morning. A crowd had gathered as word had spread rapidly across Fitzgerald about the special guest that #101 would bring to town.

It was well known that the president had taken a great interest in Warm Springs, near Manchester, and had a retreat near the springs, with their warm, healing waters. Col. Bugg had known Franklin Roosevelt as they had both been officers in the World War in Europe. This friendship had endured through the post-war years and Roosevelt's bout with infantile paralysis.

The train "sailed" into the station right on time. I remember the engineer as he lived across the street from us. He was Paul Repard.

I was standing on the concrete window ledge so I could see over the grown people who had crowded around. The office car in which the dignitaries traveled came to a smooth halt. My father took me on his shoulders as I held the roses, wrapped in green florist tissue.

As the dust of the roadbed settled, our welcome party made its way over to the rear coach of the train. The door was opened. Col. Bugg made his appearance on the vestibule with his secretary, to be joined by a big man in a wheelchair, pushed by a valet in a white uniform, followed closely by two secret service men.

Col. Bugg introduced his guest to a roar of applause. The mayor gave a short welcome and my father stepped forward, me still seated on his shoulders, and I handed the president the roses from our garden.

The valet took the flowers. The president flashed his famous smile and thanked us, then made a short talk about better times to come. Then he was gone, just as he had arrived, in a cloud of dust and black smoke.

Across the street and back to the corner of Grant and Central on the north side is a landmark two-story building, built by the early masons to last many years. It has an inscription up high which says "1897"—a long time ago.

This fine example of period architecture is occupied by the Fitzgerald Hardware Company. You name it, if they don't have it, they will get it for you. Mr. John "Little John" Dorminy and his capable wife, Elene, operate the business, along with a variety of other real estate and farm ventures.

The office for this operation occupies a portion of the ground floor beside a side door opening onto North Grant St. I would not hesitate to say this door is the most used entry in downtown Fitzgerald. The cement steps that mount to this portal are worn down an inch or so by the shoes of workmen, bankers, electricians, plumbers, advice seekers, beggars, farmers, loggers, competing bootleggers, roofers, bakers, candlestick makers, mule skinners, blacksmiths, bill payers and collectors and lads needing

BBs for their rifles, fish hooks or maybe even a rod and reel. Harry Forbes is head clerk. There isn't a nut or bolt out or plumbing fixture that he doesn't know about and his advice about how to repair anything but a broken heart is yours for the asking. He is the son of the highly respected seamstress, Ma Forbes, with whom I acquainted you earlier in our stroll.

D. Prescott is next to Harry, a dedicated young man. If a problem arises about the location of an item or what happened or when something happened, a call echoes through the building: "I.B." And a large, soft-spoken warehouse man, I.B. Harmon, appears. He must have been born in this hardware emporium. He is troubleshooter, delivery man, solver of all problems. Maybe even Mr. Dorminy depends on him for advice, I don't know.

Carlton Birch, James Griffin and Bill Mashburn are also a pleasure to do business with. Several electricians work out of this store. J.H. "Jimmie" Haines and his stepson, Bill Beddingfield, are at your service and some young "shirt-tail" fellow, Tony Sheppard, was not too far away. (These men purchased their supplies at Fitzgerald Hardware and anyone needing an electrician, could get in touch with one by stopping by the hardware store.)

Dennis Helms is a hard-working plumber who makes his headquarters here, along with his brother "Dub" and never-tiring wife, Sarah, all good, hard-working people.

Mr. Dorminy has an inner office with a big steel safe partitioned away from the general office. His bookkeeper and clerks are Mr. Davis and Mrs. Romine Gibbs. Later, Mr. Harry Greer will be a fixture here. Mrs. Elene Dorminy was office manager.

Mr. Dorminy is never idle. He is an educated man, but he has learned much of his wisdom on the streets and the farms that surround the town. He is a keen observer. Nothing passes his eye. He could have possessed a doctoral degree in business administration, law, psychology, civil engineering and music.

There he goes now, in his little 1938 Chevy coupe, just ticking along. He is quite a young man. I have voted him most likely to succeed.

Let's say goodbye to Fitzgerald Hardware and its impressive old building. I hope time will be kind to it. Maybe someday somebody will comment, "This historic old building is worth saving." And it is. But please don't cover up the side door! It will surely be haunted by the multitude of laughing, sweating, just-glad-to-be-alive humanity that tried to wrest a living from a developing land.

Mr. Dorminy will be remembered in the future for his helping hand to these people with loans, jobs and, last but not least, advice. Wish I had taken more that he gave me. Sail on, John.

As we move on down East Central, we come to the entrance of the Southern Sales Grocery Store, Jessie D. Powell, proprietor. This is another old-fashioned general store with brooms and mops, brand-new oak rocking chairs, a crate of live chickens and some half-dead onion sets. These stores kind of sleep through the week days, but come to life on the weekend, mostly with the rural crowd.

It is much like Johnny's store, where we lingered too long. The two stores face each other across the broad street with its plaza park.

Next door, as we move along the battered sidewalk—watch your step!—a newcomer, Mr. Freeman, and his brother-in-law, a young man just returned from the war, Sam Frank Glenn, have opened a store called Freeman's Seed and Feed, carrying a full line of crop seeds, animal feeds and farm chemicals, like DDT and Toxafine to kill boll weevils on cotton, the scourge of the cotton farmer. The new insecticides are much more efficient than catching the little buggers by hand and dropping them in a drink bottle of kerosene. Good luck, fellows. These "boys" impress me. That one named Sam Glenn seems hell-bent to succeed. .

We have reached the mid-block alley and the rest of the block is well occupied by the Planters Cotton Warehouse and Loan Company, buyers of cotton, makers of crop loans, dealers in fertilizers and chemicals. John Henry Dorminy is president.

Mr. Grayly (Eugene G.) Hale and his handsome son James hold forth as general manager and assistant. This is one of the major industries of this area. The railroad's switch tracks branch into the rear of this sprawling warehouse with the creaking heart pine floors. Its many sliding doors open directly into the box cars parked adjacent. I believe I hear the little ol' black steam-powered switch engine lining up the cars to proper doors. J.M. "Bear" Mathis and his crew are knocking off the hand brakes and being sure no gangplanks are still positioned in the open doors and that no kids have hitched a ride in the open cars.

'These railroad cars are loaded with bulk fertilizer, potash, nitrate of soda, phosphoric sand, etc. The Planters Warehouse has the facilities to custom mix fertilizers for retail sale to individual farmers. Man alive, when these chemicals are mixed with guano and sulfur fumes, with the black smoke from that old switch engine—we don't need to tarry back here.

Many high school lads have had their first taste of labor down in the mixing hole at 35¢ an hour. It's a wonder they even survived, much less grew on up. Buck up, fellows. See you at the Spotted Pig. A good cold bottle of beer sure will cut that fertilizer crud out of your throats. Fellows, become doctors, lawyers or maybe even used car salesmen. Many present citizens of Fitzgerald and Atlanta, maybe even New York City, started their difficult struggle up the stairway to success from this pit.

Let's say goodbye to Bear Mathis and his switch crew, Carl Furlong, Butch Whittle, Engineer John Mullis and Fireman John Wright. Shovel the coal into that firebox, John. The town needs a good smoking! I do hope you boys have satisfied Grayly Hale and the railroad agent, Ted Dunn, pedaling away on a bicycle. When are you going to buy you a car, Ted? Who in the world can guess who that "kid boy" is, sitting on Ted's handlebars?

Let's dust off and regroup. Stayed too long again, didn't we?

I do want to tell you about the hundreds of bales of cotton that will be lined along the sidewalk and even into the brick street, leaving only one narrow lane for westbound traffic. This array of bales, with their steel bands containing the fluttery white mass of cotton, are clothed in jute bagging, each with a slash exposing a puff of white cotton where the grader has taken his sample to determine the staple length and foreign matter content so important to the price the farmer will receive. Yes, they look like an army standing at mute attention.

In fact, after leaving Mr. Dorminy's gin, these fresh-ginned bales are parked here outside the warehouse to see if any of them are going to catch fire. Several bales are scattered in the park, blackened and smoking. This is an annual event in downtown Fitzgerald, every September, October and November—a little inconvenience, but a lot of hard-earned money is at stake.

We live by the golden rule here in Georgia: the ones who have the gold make the rules; the others can bump thunder until they get some gold! I could be wrong. Just a thought.

(If the moisture was too high in the cotton when it was baled, the bales could spontaneously combust. There was no problem with cotton that had not been compressed. The bales were placed outside the warehouse so that if they did burn, they wouldn't take the warehouse with them.

When a bale started burning, the fire wouldn't be visible, only smoke, because the burning would be inside. If a bale started smoking, firefighters would come from the firehouse down the street, cut the steel bands and tear open the bale to put out the fire. Paul says that cotton was brought to the gin in bulk quantities, and a suction pipe sucked the cotton out of the truck and out to the gin. A man who stood in the truck and raked cotton toward the pipe with his feet told Paul that the suction made his toes tremble and that it kept his feet cool and was like getting a foot massage at the same time. A bale of cotton weighed 500 lbs. and Paul's wife, Gladys ,remembers that for farm children, picking cotton was often a way to earn money for school clothes. At a rate of a penny a pound, a picker had to pluck a lot of light, fluffy cotton bolls to make any money at all.)

We are going to have to cross the double-lane street and visit the thriving business on the south side of Central Avenue, down on the corner of Central and Sherman Street.

This half block is interesting in the development of the Colony City. The first business, I have to inform you, is as doomed as river steamers and animal-drawn vehicles. The dusty old store is Audie Shepard's harness shop. It smells of neat's-foot oil, leather and chewing tobacco. Audie is a large man, sitting in an ancient swivel chair at a still older roll-top desk. He is asleep at present, but will spring to life and fix you right up with a hoss collar, bridle, different kinds of bits, hames, plow lines, even a little saddle for a boy's Shetland pony. Aubrey has a very attractive wife. Wonder how he got "hitched" to such a splendid woman? (The 1937 City Directory has Audie Shepard's harness shop at 215 E. Central, with a blacksmith, Clinton Robbins, occupying the rear of the building.)

I believe I see Inez Bridges dipping ice cream in

Kimball's Ice Cream Parlor and, folks, she is an expert at constructing a double-dip cone nearly as beautiful as she is. I do hope nice places like this will survive the changes that loom on the horizon.

OK, get ready for a change right now. The rest of the block is automotive, with one notable exception, the McClain Sisters' Sandwich Shop, a "hand out" cafe right on the sidewalk. Best chicken salad sandwich in town. Any town. (As Paul remembers it, customers didn't go inside McClain's, but the sandwiches were passed out to them through a sliding window. Some Fitzgerald High School students walked to McClain's from school for lunch—the high school had no cafeteria at the time—and some recall eating inside. The building was a small stand, Paul says, about the size of a school bus.)

In this stretch of sidewalk are workshops. Bill Walker and Grover Kearce are busy rebuilding car batteries and recapping tires, a recycling operation that tends to pollute the air, but these boys can save you some real money with a "pretty good" product. Don't see how Bill's wife can stay so fresh and pretty as she works as secretary-treasurer amid the acid fumes and "cooking" rubber.

On the corner of Central Avenue and Sherman Street is a landmark business, Paul Stone's filling station, dealing in independent gas, oil and tractor fuel. Paul has over-the-road tanker trucks that go down to Port St. Joe, Fla., fill up and come back to his bulk station down on Meade Street where the railroad siding also accommodates railroad tank cars. All through the war, Paul managed to supply the vital farming operations that by now have quite a few tractors that operate on gasoline and a low-grade fuel.

(During the war, to conserve fuel, some tractors ran on kerosene. They were cranked with gasoline and run until the engine had heated up, then changed over to "tractor fuel," which cost about half as much as the gasoline.)

Oil, tires and batteries, all were rationed to regular citizens, but farmers were more or less exempt. We depended on them for food and fiber. Mules were still important, but look out! The county is resounding to the put-put-put-put of those infernal "one lung" John Deere tractors, turning that black dirt over while the plow man sits in a metal seat, bouncing along instead of hopping over clods with a plow line strung around his neck.

Paul Stone's truck, driven by Wiley Luke, delivers fuel to the skid tanks at farms in the county, pouring smelly diesel or kerosene to quench the never-ending thirst of these steel behemoths, Ford 8N's, Farmall models M, H, C and A ("A" was the smallest) and Cubs and those popping old John Deeres. (Farmers had gas tanks on skids, so they could get the tank to wherever the tractor was when it needed refueling.)

Move over, Maude and Bell, you have been good and faithful servants, but the bell has tolled for you hay burners. You mules next in the lot, you may get to pull tobacco sleds or maybe even plow some garden.

Paul Stone is able to "carry" or credit the farmers. They more or less depend on him and his faithful staff: Mr. Tom Smith, Tommy Pickard, bookkeeper, "Speedy" Paulk, truck driver, along with Mr. Bing; Johnny Beck, Kelly Sumner and Bill Hargett change, repair and mount literally mountains of tires while Paul Stone walks around lighting that crooked-stemmed pipe. Some people say he must have been born with it in his mouth. Maybe someday he will manage to build himself a new station. This one has really outgrown itself. Tommy Pickard's office is stacked to the roof with new tires, all sizes.

Let's move on. Careful, don't trip over that tire tool Kelly left lying there.

Looking down South Sherman Street to the alley is Mr. George Gray's old livery stable. Once a place, in colony days, where a traveling salesman or young man wishing to take his darling for a buggy ride could rent a fine horse and a "rig." Now Mr. Gray stores furniture and moves people's household goods, using a truck instead of a wagon. He is a drayman. There is no one around, so we will look across the street to see the office of Dr. Marsh, a veterinarian who moved here from Atlanta some years back. Besides being a "hoss doctor," he is state inspector for milk producers, abattoirs, etc. He inspects carcasses before they are cut up, the meat saws and general conditions at abattoirs and goes to dairies to run bacteria counts on the milk. This information comes out in the paper every week. I believe I see his twin boys, William and Plyde, unloading a quantity of brown glass jugs from Doc's car, stained with that blue medicine all vets rely on to cure animal ailments. Don't spill any of that stuff on the sidewalk, boys.

The large, two-story brick building that faces Central Avenue houses Holland Davis Furniture Store, with storage upstairs. Lots of "new" couples are getting married since the men have come home from the war and setting up housekeeping around town. The furniture business is quite active. That is Charles "Chicken" Wilson standing in the door waiting for the next customer. That boy loves fried chicken!

Let's cross Sherman Street, if we can get a green light, and continue down the south side of Central Avenue. After Davis Furniture comes Bryant Brothers Mercury car dealership and repair shop. Dick and Lorenzo Bryant, local boys who had rather work on cars than eat when they are hungry, are under car hoods while Lamar Davis and Lanier McEwen are busy aligning front ends and changing oil and doing lube jobs.

Allen Royal, retired railroad shop worker and good all-around fellow, with his bull dog, has just come in from his daily walk, felt hat setting at an angle on his bald head.

He should live to be 100, if walking is good for you. The old dog is tired and is sound asleep, oblivious to the racket these mechanics are making. Busy place.

Bryant Brothers also introduced, sells and services Cushman scooters, which have gone over big in Fitzgerald. They are well designed, well built motor-driven, serviceable, easy to crank machines that anyone can operate. They are colorful, quiet and affordable. A Cushman will run and run on a gallon of gas, but the top speed is 35 or 40 miles per hour. They are very convenient uptown. No parking problem. The town is full of them, mostly owned by high school students, but a good number of adults also.

At one time period, shortly after World War II, a young man could scarcely get a date with a girl unless he had a Cushman. When the movie is over at 10 p.m., you should hear the scooters being cranked by kick starters. The girls sit side-saddle on the "buddy seat." Look out! They are headed for the Spotted Pig, out on South Grant Street, to have a hamburger and milk shake. Get ready, Emma Sue Drummond, here they come.

Even the railroad "call boys" zip around the neighborhoods calling train crews for their runs on the Atlanta, Birmingham and Coast Railroad. There goes John Morris, crew clerk, on his scooter with his call book in his overall hip pocket. Each crew member, conductor, engineer, fireman, brakeman and flagman will have to sign John's book to confirm the time of the call and show up for duty. You do understand that Fitzgerald with the "yards" at Westwood is a terminal, or crew change point. This business district probably wouldn't exist as it is today, if it weren't for the AB&C.

Thanks, Bryant Brothers, for the Cushman scooter. They put a lot of people on wheels who would have been walking or pedaling bicycles. They are great, except on rainy, cold nights, when maybe you can borrow your dad's auto if you are lucky and have gas money.

Let's say goodbye to the brothers Bryant and all the satisfied customers, past and present, who gather here.

If we may cast our eyes across Central, over to the north side, we see the brick building that sits firmly on the corner of Sherman Street and Central Avenue. It is the fire department and city hall, also the new jail that takes the complex to the mid-block alley. A few comments on this location will hardly suffice to do justice to its importance to the city.

I don't know the date it was constructed, but it was probably built soon after the colony was set in motion. The first fire-fighting equipment, the horse-drawn pump wagons and the water tank wagon, are still stored here. Wade Cleary is chief and a big American La France fire truck sits polished and tuned to perfection by the full-time firefighters, among whom are Webster Dix, Willie Crawford, Ed and Gene Davis, Wayne Sherrill, Mr. C. Rawlins, Dean Mitchum and others, all ready to slide down the pole that reaches to the upstairs wardroom, or living quarters. A loud siren that sits on the roof sounds when a fire call comes in. Man, that thing can be heard for miles, as the boys climb aboard and Chief Cleary starts the engine and rings the shining brass bell.

That may be a spotted Dalmatian dog sitting next to Wade and Dean, who is firmly clenching a stub of cigar between his teeth. These men have a commendable fire control record. It may be the best in the state. Don't get in their way!

Next door is the "water and light" office. The city clerk is Julius Bailey. His staff, poring over the record books, are Mrs. Jim Weaver and Miss Beauchamp, who is to become Chief Cleary's bride. It is a busy office, as the citizens of Fitzgerald—the affluent ones, that is, who have running water and electricity—pay their monthly bills. My mother like to have fainted recently when her bill went over $3. That meter reader must have made a mistake.

City taxes are paid here. Lord, what are things coming to, but taxes must be paid, or Julius will turn the bills over to the constable and you will find yourself paying a fine.

Upstairs is the city council meeting hall, overseen by Mayor Alvin Brown, the postman who had the pony named Billy that knew this fair city like a book, as he drew the mail cart through the streets, rain or shine, freeze or storm, for more years than I can remember.

Alvin is a great mayor, being one of the Northern colonists who came here in the beginning.

For years Fitzgerald has needed a new jail. Now we have a fine modern facility. There aren't many occupied cells as people here seldom need locking up. Chief Gordon Roberts, Sgt. George Crawford, Linus Paul, Milton Finley, the "speed cop," Tom Myers, Shorty Grantham, Joe Fussell, Speedie Paulk on his motorcycle, Furman Stone and Nathan Pope, to name a few. Their very appearance would quell any thoughts of misbehavior. They sure deserve a better station than the little cellar that I will point out to you later on in our stroll through town.

I am tired of crossing back and forth across this wide Central Avenue and only another cotton warehouse occupies the half block that goes to Sheridan Street, the Ben Hill Warehouse. It is a cotton storage, fertilizer and seed, sales and loan company that has everything farmers need to make a crop.

This agricultural business is owned by one of the most prominent citizens, J.J. "Capt. Jack" Dorminy, a legend in his own time, farming, producing seed oil and fertilizer, operating saw mills and also involved in naval stores. His was a prominent family in this area when Mr. Fitzgerald dreamed up this city. Capt. Jack is a Southern gentleman who represented the Southern or "rebel" faction of this experimental Yank-Reb city. His grandson, Jack

Massee, is manager and W.H. Robitzsch is chief clerk-manager. Wilmer Dorminy is also associated with this warehouse. Reuben Branam is the warehouse man.

A great place to sit down and visit, but we must move on. I hardly realized Fitzgerald has grown so much and is so big.

Let's cross the alley here on the south side of Central Avenue to find ourselves in front of a large masonry building that has a runway or alley of its own right through the middle. The rear looks like an open barn, which it is, because it is George Boney's mule barn. Mr. Boney is another prominent Southern businessman about Ben Hill County. Mules soon replaced the draft horses that the Yankees brought down from the North and Midwest, but they were not acclimated to the hot, humid weather of south Georgia and soon were replaced by the tough, hard-working mules from Tennessee, Oklahoma and Missouri.

Mr. Boney, who was raised near the Ocmulgee River around China Hill (China Hill is on the Telfair side of the Ocmulgee, around Milan.) probably knows more about livestock than anyone, along with being a sharp trader, came to the front when Mr. J.L. Perry died suddenly. Mr. Perry was the original mule trader from Oklahoma, who came here in colony days. His death left an open field for Mr. Boney.

Mr. Boney cuts quite a figure in his $100 blue suit, pearl gray felt Stetson hat and Florsheim shoes shined until he can see his face in them and a fly swatter to swat the flies away. He is a gentleman farmer and owns a large herd of purebred, white-faced Hereford cattle. He deals in all sorts of animals, even milk cows and riding horses. His handlers break young stock in the alley way, which is lined with pens occupied by all classes of stock, even a billy goat that relishes the few weeds that spring up around the premises. We won't go behind the building, but on the back alley is a blacksmith's shop, a Mecca for loafers and retirees. Don't misunderstand me, it is a busy place. No office, no safe, just a shed, no spreading oak tree, but here is the village smithy, Mr. Cook. He can shoe a horse or mule, his clanging hammer can shape a red-hot piece of steel or iron into any shape a customer wants—listen to it sizzle as Mr. Cook plunges it into a vat of water to cool and temper the desired object. Now, that steel isn't all that sizzles. The old men argue politics and ball games while another group carefully studies their hands of cards at the pinochle game that is always in progress.

Mr. Boney and his nephew, John C., are lenient, shall we say, about boys with BB guns who shoot pigeons and sparrows that nest in the barn loft, sometimes raiding a nest for baby pigeons or squabs. As long as you behave, Mr. Boney never sees you.

I hope this great business is always here for the farmers and kids and a wonderful "senior center" for the political analysts and card sharks who play for match stems and bottle crowns.

Let's move on. Wait, I do believe John C. Boney is building a used car lot on his Uncle George's vacant lot. Is that the knell of the bell of the future I hear ringing? Good luck, John C.

Next on the corner of Central and Sheridan, across from the courthouse, is Roland Stone's service station, dealers in gas and oil. Is that John Hughes working there, servicing his pulpwood trucks? This pulpwood business is booming since the war. It probably won't last long, as the old heads tell me that the pulp wooders will soon cut out the pine forest around here. They won't last long at the rate they are hauling it off. Why every southbound train has 10 or 15 cars loaded high, headed for Brunswick or Savannah paper mills. Maybe we are witnessing a new industry with many jobs, for our thriving town that has long depended on the railroad and cotton mill for its lifeblood.

While we stand on this corner, we can look across Central Avenue and see several businesses that have been around since settlement days. In the 400-block is one of the early granitoid cement block houses that dot the residential sections of Fitzgerald. It is still a home. Next, extending to the mid-block alley, is another brick cotton warehouse, much like the ones we saw west of here. It is the Central Warehouse, owned by the Paulk family. It is managed by Reason Paulk and buys, stores and trades in cotton, fertilizer and seed. (The 1937-38 City Directory shows the Central Warehouse was owned by Drew Paulk. It was located at 408 E. Central. At that time, Reason Paulk was manager of the Ben Hill Company.)

You do understand that behind these warehouses, the tracks of the AB&C Railroad connect these tradesmen to all parts of world trade. They load cotton bound for Liverpool, England, Kobe, Japan and Yokohama. Fertilizer arrives in box cars from all over the world right here in our city of brotherly love.

On to the east is a landmark business, the Standard Supply Company, founded when Fitzgerald was known as Shack Town. An enterprising Yankee lad by the name of Jim Parrott arrived here from the cold, windswept state of Iowa. He told me, with his own mouth, that he was a fireman on a steam locomotive in the north and he got tired of chopping up ice with an axe to furnish the boiler with water. He heard of the Fitzgerald colony and caught the first thing smoking to the sun-kissed state of Georgia. He was truly a founding father and a skilled builder—building many of the buildings I am pointing out to you today, including the one I was born in.

He can still be seen around his shop, busy as a bee. He must be 90 years old now. He never complains of being tired or discouraged, a great role model for the young men. He was blessed with two capable sons, Harold and Lauren, who have now taken the reins of this fine business.

Below here, too far for us foot-sore pilgrims to walk, is Bennie Anderson's Dixie peanut mill. Jake Miller is foreman of the shelling operation. Mr. Cherry is warehouse foreman and Rex McEwen is bookkeeper. They possibly load out 100 railroad cars of peanuts and employ many women in the shelling and grading plant.

Below Thomas Street is the St. James Hotel, now slipping into disrepair. But it was one of the first hotels or rooming houses during colony days. Below the hotel is Mrs. Fox's "Happy Home." She is another founder of Fitzgerald. (Paul has a soft spot in his heart for Mrs. Fox. She raised rat terriers and gave him a puppy when he was a boy. "You never forget that," he says.)

Wyman's Grocery was across the street on Central, in an ancient building, now occupied by Mr. R.E. Lee, a pecan buyer. Wake up, Mr. Lee, buy this bag of nuts. Your old scales are getting rusty.

Time marches on, folks, and we must, also.

Sitting proudly in the middle of the neighborhood that I have just shown you sits the Ben Hill County Courthouse. There must have been some craftsmen in those early days, to erect such a building. Mr. Parrott told me he built it. He must have had lots of help.

You all know the activities and offices in the courthouse. Several of the original officers are still at their post. My favorite is the clerk of the court, David Paulk, with his secretary, Miss Frances Tanner. No one will ever call the roll of jurors with the style and aplomb that Mr. Paulk can. He knows nearly every citizen by his first name, and the ones he doesn't know, he just calls them "John Henry," if they are male, and if they are female he calls them "Mary Jane." Stay on the job forever, Mr. Paulk! Also here are Henry Evans, tax receiver, and Mrs. Graham, tax collector.

Virgil Griner is sheriff and John Smith is jailer. Last but not least is the custodian of this elegant, if not aging, building, with its generous dome and stalwart columns. He is a wiry, ageless type man by the name of Mr. Greer.

Each office is heated by a coal stove, which has to be kindled and started each morning. All winter, he is here at dawn and has the fire roaring. He is also a handy man and helps on court days. Great job, Mr. Greer.

One reason everybody is so nice hereabouts is that ugly old brick jail house at the corner of Sheridan and Pine that grimly rises two stories high, with lightning rods pointing straight to heaven. The top story is cells, with their black iron bars at every window. Downstairs is where the sheriff and his family have made their home.

Be good, folks, or you may end up behind those grim bars, hollering to passersby to bail you out. But the passersby seem to be deaf. There may be some pitiful wife with a baby in her arms and a brood of young'uns clinging to her skirts. Sad, but true.

Across from the jail is a large pecan tree which affords good shade and a gathering place for black day laborers who are seeking work for the day. If you want a job, be under the tree at day break and be sure to have your lunch bucket.

Oh, well, let's move on from the corner of Pine and Sheridan streets. We will move west on East Pine Street.

As we make the turn, John Hurt's auto garage is in the ancient galvanized tin barn that is beginning to rust. We might even call it an eyesore, but it serves well as a repair garage. Mr. Hurt is a good repairman and can tune up your "old bus." He kept many an old flivver and pickup running during the war, with hay wire and junk parts.

The old barn is a little colorful, though. Fletcher Fussell has plastered circus and carnival bills on the rusting exterior, with arrival dates on them. There is one for "Celebrities Circus," Clyde Beatty defying a roaring lion, Silas Green from New Orleans, James E. Straight's

Carnival.   Then there are the medicine signs: 666, Midol, Vick's Salve and Gillette razors.   You tried hard, Fletcher, to dress the old girl up.   He might even hand out a few free passes if we see him around.

Near here, John C. "Preacher" Taylor once had a store, selling mostly fish from a small block building in the alley parallel to Pine Street.

Across the street is Elder Hollingsworth's ice plant. We might step over and get a drink from his perpetual ice water fountain.   It's free. Elder Hollingsworth also sells coal, which is delivered by the ton to houses. (According to the 1950 City Director, Elder Hollingsworth owned Crystal Ice Company at 323 E. Pine St. and was president of Central Motor Service. The "ice water fountain" was a pipe that released water chilled by the ice-making process.)

Ahead lie two blocks that just could be the most interesting stretch of street in Fitzgerald. This is where the action is, believe me.

These streets are red brick, by the way. A rich, red color. They were hand laid by large groups of Italian brick layers who went all over the U.S. building such brick streets. They lived in tent camps and had their own cooks and attendants. They spoke no English and were happy to have a job. My father told me of them. Just thought you might like to know who did all this labor.

The streets have probably held up much better than the skilled hands that laid them so carefully. You realize, that was 50-odd years ago now, my weary tourist.   If sidewalks could talk, they could tell you more stories than I could ever begin to in the next 50 years to come. But maybe I can hit on the high spots.

Street characters abound here, especially on Saturdays, until midnight.   Hole-in-the-wall businesses also abound. Black and white merchants thrive side by side. Dry cleaning "clubs" or "pressing clubs" clean and block hats, steam-press suits and dresses and do alterations and patch clothes. Good, honest black men and their wives—to name two, John M. Edge with his Sunshine Dry Cleaning and James Edge at City Dry Cleaning Co. (The 1937-38 City Directory lists Sunshine Dry Cleaning at 118 S. Sherman and City Dry Cleaning at 117-119 S. Sherman. Both businesses later moved to Pine Street, Sunshine to 315 E. Pine and City to 407 E. Pine.)

Clean piles of Sunday best clothes, suits altered for the Jewish merchants are here. The steam presses hiss as the operators, stripped to their undershirts, glistening with good honest sweat, press the foot pedal that raises and lowers the cloth-lined press as their deft hands arrange the clothing to be pressed. The top press comes down and the steam billows out, all around the operator and the "club." They even pick up and deliver, all over town. Big business! There are fish markets and taxi stands. There is "Mud Cat," Artis Keller, standing in front of his taxi. There isn't a street or alley he doesn't know, all over town. Don't go to the city register for information. Go to Mud Cat. I do wish he would get him some store-bought front teeth, or "china clippers" as they are known hereabout. Harvey Hendricks also has a cab stand here. He worked for the railroad until his feet got to hurting him too much, and now he drives a cab.

There are meat markets, barber shops, pool rooms, all catering to a black clientele. The business that anchors this block is Bryant's second-hand store and shoe repair shop. Mr. Buster Bryant sells and buys used clothing. You can find any clothing item, to fit any budget or price range. There are even some new work clothes. Some of the items are pure rummage, but a fellow down on his luck can sell his good clothes and leave in "get by" clothes, with a couple of dollars in hand or maybe just 50¢ in his pockets. Better check the pockets for holes, my friend.

Just a few years back, people would get nice new clothes for Christmas gifts, you know. They would come down and swap them for overalls and brogans, then everyone was happy. Buster!

This block is, as they call it in New York, the "tenderloin" of Fitzgerald. Never a dull moment! I hope it will last as long as the brick streets and cracked sidewalks do. Fellow, can't you read that sign that plainly states, "Don't spit on the sidewalk"?

Before we leave the East Pine area, I must mention Riggs' Funeral Home, at 312 E. Pine, which faithfully serves the black community. It is owned by George Riggs, a prominent businessman. (This funeral home, located at 415 E. Pine, served the black community.)

Frank and Ethel Wentz (603 E. Pine) have long operated boarding houses and "clubs" that offer great meals of soul food and rooms to itinerants and workmen. A lot of railroad men from Manchester and Brunswick stay here when they stop in Fitzgerald. Florence Whipple also has a club frequented by workmen. Great job, ladies.

Other businesses along E. Pine during this period include the grocery store at 309 E. Pine owned by Eula Lamar and, later, Eldin Crawford, the People's Cafe at 317 E. Pine owned by Wesley Akridge, the Royal Steam Pressing Co., originally owned by St. Clair Coffee and later by George Washington and Johnny Moton at 313 E. Pine, lunchrooms owned by Elizabeth B. Swain at 312 1/2 E. Pine and Albirtha Paulk at 311 E. Pine, Flora Hunter's beauty shop at 309 1/2 E. Pine and barber shops owned by Charles W. McDonald and James W. Bell. Dr. Harry P. Elligan had an office at 309 1/2 E. Pine, as did Dr. Edward L. Toomer at an earlier time. In 1937, there were lunchrooms owned by Ross Hardaway (314 E. Pine), Lessie Jones (312 E. Pine) and Sallie Lee (311 1/2), as well as Julius Love's Rainbow Grill at 311 E. Pine. The Afro-American Life Insurance Co. and Pilgrim Health and Life had offices above Eula Lamar's grocery. In the 300-block of East Pine, specialty businesses owned by both black and white people were intermingled.

As the "grand tour" proceeds west on Pine Street, let's give a wave to the folks at John Owens' grocery store. Fancy grocers and a meat market, among the best.

Robitzsch Hardware Co. is next, on the corner of Sherman and Pine (202-204 E. Pine), one of the busiest corners uptown, especially for pedestrian traffic. On Saturday nights, the sidewalks won't hold the people on foot.

We have already talked about Bryant's store. Smith's Fish Market is on the corner (120 S. Sherman). This used to be a busy place on Thursday, Friday and Saturday, the fish monger's. You pick the ones you want from the ice-filled showcase. The lady weighs them, then "Peanut" Scruggs can scale and gut them right before your eyes. Mullet fish, 12¢ a pound. I would hate to see the pile of fish he has cleaned since he started work here.

Behind here is a small building facing Sherman Street. It is Carter's Cleaners. John and Martha Carter, newcomers here from Albany, are nice people who are doing a great business since the war is over. John is an avid photographer on the side. William Hageman is their pickup and delivery man. Really, he is just a kid.

Next to Eldin Crawford's grocery is Levy Claude Renfroe's Central Music Company, suppliers of jukeboxes, pinball machines, records, etc.

On the corner is Robitzsch Hardware—Martin Robitzsch, owner and operator, deals in fence wire, plumbing supplies, nails, guns, sporting items and has a show window and main entrance on Pine Street with a side door on Sherman. Shem Murray is chief clerk. Bill Robitzsch, Martin's son, finds plenty to do, and his sister, Thedessia Heys, is bookkeeper-clerk. A great team.

These streets hold many memories for me. When I was but a lad in the early thirties, Martin cleared out his show window, that had the plate glass window along the sidewalk. He then used chicken wire to fence in the back side, then "faked" a wooden scene, with stumps and palmetto palms, sand and a pool of water. Then he stocked it with diamondback and canebrake rattlesnakes.

Yes, you heard me, great big, healthy snakes, in a very natural setting. Great display, Martin. If the chamber of commerce gave a ribbon, you should be holding a blue one.

I was about 5 years old. My mom and dad were both in bed sick with the flu and a black woman by the name of Maebell was my nurse. She would always take me for a walk down East Pine Street. That day, a circus had come to town and, as usual, a parade came to the uptown streets and paraded their clowns, brass band in ill-fitting, wrinkled uniforms, trapeze aerialists, Fat Lady, Thin Man, jugglers, sword swallowers, fire eaters, Wild Man from Denver, Wild West riders, trick dogs, ringmasters, bearded woman, prancing horses, dwarves, tumblers, elephants, monkeys, lions and tigers with trainers, dancing girls, tattooed man and woman and various freaks from around the world, right here on East Pine Street. Fletcher Fussell would be in the owner's carriage.

I was terrified by Cole Brothers clowns, but I loved the coiled rattlers with their rattles singing away.

Maebell had to drag me away. My nose was flat and dirty from being pressed against the window. What an October afternoon.

Across the street is Homer Waters' old garage and filling station. Dot Waters used to pump gas here wearing high heel pumps and a sun-back dress and long, dangling earrings—a beautiful girl. O.W. Fletcher has bought the historic but dilapidated old building and is remodeling it for his own feed store and his never-ending line of goods that he trades for.

He is even getting into the new craze, air conditioning. Whoever heard of conditioning the air? It is now in several buildings around town, like the Grand Theatre. No telling what O.W. will come up with next. He is quite an entrepreneur. It is said that he could sell an electric fan to an Eskimo. I don't know about that. But he would sure try. No joke, he is one of our best businessmen and just a great person to be around. Homer Waters, character that he was, would look down and give one of his belly laughs if he knew O.W. Fletcher now operated his old headquarters. Let's all join in and laugh with him.

Our attention is back to the corner of East Pine and South Sherman, looking north on Sherman to the mid-block alley, the turn-back point of our tour of East Central Avenue. Dr. A.B. Griner keeps a veterinary office along here, but he is gone most of the time, "patching" up old and sick horses, mules, dogs and other pets. He is very active in and formed the earliest Garden Club in the city, and has much knowledge of camellia culture and skills in grafting and budding these beautiful shrubs. His home on S. Main Street is one of the show places of the town from Christmas until spring. Thanks "Doc" Griner.

For many years Fred Hughes operated a popular grocery store and meat market here on Sherman Street.

Going to the mid-block alley is one of Fitzgerald's best known combination fish and seafood markets and cafes. Clean as a whistle, side door on the alley leading to the kitchen and a table set to feed anyone a fine fish or oyster dinner at a reasonable price. Miss Beulah Dykes and her sister know their cooking.

Is that Wootsen Goff cleaning mullet fish at that long galvanized sink?

Up front is the main dining room. Yes, my friends, you may see the richest or the poorest citizens mixing and meeting at McCall's Fish Market. Good job, ladies.

At the corner where we stand, Birdsey Feed Store, operated by Mr. Streetman, does a thriving business in feed, seed and chicken biddies. The front entrance faces

Pine Street and a long brick wall fronts the sidewalk along Sherman Street. It faces east and catches the morning sun. This sunny, protected spot is a favorite spot for the street people and homeless souls who bask in the sun on cool mornings. It's kind of a senior center. You can hear sad stories, learn a little history of the settlement of Fitzgerald, learn how to roll a tailor-made cigarette, bum a dime, get a drag of 40/40 wine, get the low-down on other citizens, hear of lost fortunes, faded love stories, political news (whether you loved Franklin Roosevelt or hated him), conditions at the jail, when more WPA surplus groceries would be handed out or complain about how dull the needle was that the health nurse gave the last typhoid shot with. The needles were seldom cleaned, only nested in a glass of rubbing alcohol.

Yes, Fitzgerald does have a skid row, and this is about as close to it as you can get.

I see Charlie Gibbs, another well known trader, leading a nice little Jersey cow by a rope and halter. He may walk 10 or 15 miles to deliver her to some family that needs milk to keep the faces rosy on 10 or 12 rural children. This area of town is Mecca for traders. You might even get a three-dollar Ingersoll pocket watch for fifty cents from some thirsty workman, if you have the fifty cents. What a street this Sherman Street is.

Back to where we stand on the west side of Sherman Street, there is no need to go further. I hate to call it "skid row," but if it isn't, it's as close as this fair city has: hole-in-the-wall storefronts, bars, or rather "beer joints," such as Carl's Bar, pawnshops, wine stores. Maybe I should say, life's other side. But who am I to judge? Every town has a district like this, some worse, mind you.

But let's go before we get our teeth "adjusted" by a flying beer bottle. You boys and girls have a good time. I love your jukeboxes, Rock-Ola Wurlitzers—a quarter in the slot will make all colors of light come on and you get five

Paul Dunn's mother (left), Tessie Myrick Dunn, and her twin sister. Mrs.Dunn is holding Paul's brother, who died in an accident as a child. Her parents were among the original colonists who founded Fitzgerald.

Paul Dunn's father, Ted (at right), is pictured with a traveling salesman at the AB&A freight depot in 1916, when he was 25 years old.

This was the dining room at Fitzgerald's famous Lee-Grant Hotel. Paul Dunn says he was about seven years old when this picture was taken, and he doesn't know what the occasion was. His parents, Tessie and Ted, are sitting to the left of the support pole at left. Tessie's hair is dark and Ted is wearing glasses. Behind Ted, closest to the left side of the pole is Sheriff Virgil Griner. Mrs. Eulalie Masssee is seated at right (behind the empty chair).

At left: Ruth Hall Burkett and Mary Jack Dixon Johnson worked at the Grand Theatre as teenagers during the period Paul Dunn about which Paul Dunn writes, selling tickets and running the concession stand after school and on the weekends. The Stone-Vinson Motors sign advertises the dealership on the next corner, where Nabila's Garden Restaurant is now. The building in the background across the street appears to be the Buice Building, then a hotel.

At right: Gerald Hardin poses with his car on E. Pine Street. In the background are Gottlieb's men's clothing store and the Fair Store. (Photo courtesy of Mildred Campbell.)

Homer Waters drives his "bucking Ford" in a 1940 parade. Seated beside him is Rachel Green. A note on the photo indicates that she lived "next to the laundry," presumably the White Swan. Occupying the buildings along the street are (from left) the Beauty Bob (prior to its move to W. Central), McCard's Jewelry and the Grand Theatre. Other business in these two blocks of S. Main Street, at the time the 1937-38 City Directory was published, included Adams Plumbing Co. and Branch Electric Co., both in the Grand building, between the box office and the corner, where the Grand Coffee Shop was located. Across the alley were Miller Furniture Company, the Vendome Grocery, plumber Hubert Roush, Rogers Stores and Henderson's Market (meat), John C. Prescott's lunch counter, Elias Lovett's barber shop and, at the corner of Central, Terminal Station, where the bus station and a service station were located.

Prior to the post-war era, in which Paul Dunn's tour is set, the whole country was involved in the war effort. Above, left, Boy Scouts (including, from left, Theo Griffin and George Eckerd, schoolmates of Paul's) collect aluminum in front of Central United Methodist Church. (Photo courtesy of Mildred Evans Griffin.)

At right: Ida Taylor is well remembered as the ticket seller at the Grand Theatre in the 1940s.

Many soldiers "hoboed" home by hopping on freight trains after they were discharged at the end of the war. Pictured is Lawrence Moorehead of Mystic, Paul Dunn's brother-in-law and the brother of Gladys Dunn and Willa Ree Tucker.

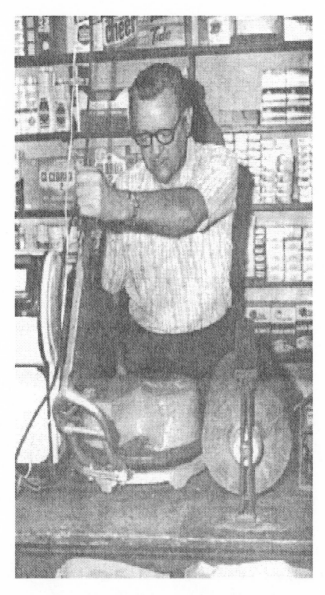

Using his by-then antique slicer, Johnnie Garrison cuts a wedge of cheese from a wheel. The grocery store was known for its hoop cheese.

At harvest time, bales of cotton filled the sidewalks in front of Planters Warehouse and overflowed into the street. Bales with high moisture content were placed outside as spontaneous combustion was a possibility.

The Fitzgerald Fire Department's 750-gallon American-La France pumper, pictured here around 1915, was still in use in the 1940s.

Standard Supply is one of Fitzgerald's oldest businesses, founded by a colonist from Iowa, Jim Parrott. At 90, he could still be found in the shop. The two-story building burned some years ago.

The Lamar family owned this grocery at 309 E. Pine, which later became Crawford's Grocery, owned by Eldin Crawford. It was one of many black-owned businesses on E. Pine Street.

In the 1940s, this building was known as the Jeff Davis Hotel, but when this picture was taken, around the turn of the last century, it was the Aldine Hotel. The crowd is gathered to support Hoke Smith in another campaign for governor.

The Fitzgerald Police Department was once housed in the basement of the old First National Bank at the corner of Grant and Pine. The railing along the Grant Street side in this picture marks the entrance. Capt. Jack Dorminy's office was at the rear of the building, at the door.

The Garbutt-Donovan building, commonly known as the Five-Story Building, dominates the skyline of East Pine Street in this picture from the 1930s or 1940s.

Dime stores like McLellan's were the Wal-Marts of their day. The store, located in the building that now houses the Colony Art Gallery, was a mainstay in downtown Fitzgerald in the forties and beyond. (Photo, taken in the 1930s by Dave Paulk, is courtesy of Margie Bryant, Mr. Paulk's granddaughter.)

Pictured in this photo, taken at the Fitzgerald Airport in 1946, are (from left) Everett Martin, Marvin Roberts, flight instructor Walter Nix, Wilson Studstill, two unidentified men, Dr. W.E. Tuggle, unidentified, Dr. John McCord, Cliff Bridges, unidentified and Homer Waters. (Photo courtesy of Jack Martin.)

This photograph, taken by Margie Bryant's grandfather, Dave Paulk, offers a rare glimpse of the Greek cafes. At right is Birdsey's, with the Rogers Store next to it. Next is the City Fruit and Lunch Room (the white building with signs across the top advertising seafood, barbecue and ice cream). This was Bill Pope's establishment at 224 E. Pine. Beyond it are Sam Abram's dry good store, Cohen's Department Store, then Nick Pope's Liberty Café at 216 E. Pine. Beyond it are Grigsby's dry good store, the Fair Store and Gottlieb's.

In this 1930s photo of Haile's, taken by Dave Paulk, signs advertise limeade for 5¢, Walgreen's aspirin for 39¢ and school supplies. The lunch counter was advertising fried chicken. A lunch plate cost a quarter. The faded sign for Mrs. Newton's dress shop can be discerned on the building at the left. (Photo courtesy of Margie Bryant.)

Janet Willingham (left) and her friend Jeanette McCook, who was nicknamed "Yep Man," posed for this 1940s snapshot. Janet bought a camera during the time she worked at the popular drugstore and took photos of her friends downtown. (Courtesy of Janet Willingham.)

The awning at left marks the Pine Street entrance to the Piedmont Hotel at the corner of Pine and Main (where the Grand Plaza Park is now). Between the hotel entrance and the C&S Store is the Georgia Motor Finance Company. This photo was taken in the 1930s by Dave Paulk. (Courtesy of Margie Bryant.)

These members of the Young businessmen's Bible Class, were among
the community leaders who shaped the Fitzgerald of the 1940s. Among
those pictured on the steps of Central United Methodist Church are
(from left): front, W. Henry Evans, president, the Rev. J. Ed Fain,
teacher, and W.E. Hoyle, secretary-treasurer; middle, E.A. Thompson
Jr., H. Grady Langley, Frank A. Cason, H. Grady McDaniel, Paul H.
Matthews, T.O. Bazemore and P. Quincy Tucker, and rear, John B.
Evans, M.H. "Duke" Massee Jr., Allan C. Garden, Sam Jones, J.L.
Phillips, Robert W. Smith, Ernest K. Justice, J. Jarratt Pryor and Ted N.
Dunn, Paul Dunn's father.

The Grand Theatre and its neighboring shop fronts are decked out in bunting, probably for the Fourth of July. *Battleground*, the film advertised on the banner hanging from the marquee, was released in 1949, dating this photograph. The plaza park in front of the theatre is completely bare of grass. A bicycle is parked in the rack in front, its rear wheel just visible behind one of the parked cars. Located in the shop buildings were (from left) the Fitzgerald Jewelry Company, the Beauty Bob Beauty Shop and, on the other side of the Grand, Pate's Sewing Machines and the office of Dr. John D. McCord. J. Clarence Hunter owned the jewelry store and Maxie Pate the sewing machine store. The Beauty Bob belonged to John Y. Brown and Alma B. McLendon.

The staff of Williams Chevrolet in the 1940s included Mr. Helton (at left in the white shirt and tie), Thelma Dixon, E.C. Mann and the Swanson brothers. (Photo courtesy of Emory C. Mann.)

Emory C. Mann was just out of high school when he went to work for Edd Evans at the Central Pharmacy. This photo was taken in 1941. Behind him can be seen signs for the funeral home and The Herald-Leader office, which used to be located in the 100-block of E. Central. (Photo courtesy of Emory C. Mann.)

Birdsey's feed store did a thriving business in feed, seed and biddies. The sunny wall along Sherman Street was a popular place for street people, too. This photo, taken in the 1930s, is courtesy of Margie Bryant.

The Manhattan Barber Shop had its heyday well before 1946, but some of these barbers were still working in the 1940s. Pictured are (from left) Doc Deese, Art Cripe, unidentified, and Burt Archer. The customers and shoeshine boy are not identified in this 1914 photograph.

songs. Most of the songs are sad: Patsy Cline's "I Fall to Pieces," Kitty Wells's "God Didn't Make Honky Tonk Angels" and "I Might as well be Talking to the Ceiling," Hank Williams's "Lovesick Blues" and others. The taxi dancers are tired, but for a dime they will come to life. Beer seems to fuel the whole thing.

We might even see you at Pop's Place or the Silver Moon after this tour.

Let's go on back up to E. Pine Street and go west, young man, go west. The founders of this town predicted it would grow to the west, and so far it has. Let's stay on the sidewalk on the north side and look across the street to the Pine Theatre, a movie house, showing westerns and second-run films, mostly on Saturday. The girls selling tickets that they tear off big yellow rolls and pop up in slots (on the other side of the window) are Ruth Hall, Jeannette Seals, LaJean Fussell and Ann Mathis. They are as pretty as lots of the actresses who ride the purple sage.

Next door is Allen's Super Market, a new innovation in grocery marketing. It won't amount to much, I don't think. Look—you just stroll around, with a buggy, find what you need, put it in the basket, with no clerk at all, then you push it to the checkout stall and unload it onto the counter and a lady tallies up your bill on the cash register, and you have to pay hard, cold cash money.

Only Owen Segraves, a fine young man, has innovated like this. No checker games, no political "analysis," no crop news, no live chickens, no prayer list, no credit ticket. Your feet are tired, you have walked a mile or more. Owen gives you a big handshake and tells us all to return next Saturday as he and his hard-working staff will be right there to serve you. Come on, Owen, you need to oil the wheels on these old buggies.

His manager, Mr. Lightsey, Mrs. Mobley and Miss Alice, the checkout girls, have been at work for 12 or 14 hours. And Owen's wife, Frances, is sitting straight up amid a roll of papers, trying to keep the books balanced. A carefree bunch of high school boys started putting up stock at daybreak and around 11 o'clock that night will be mopping up the floor, but their pay envelope will contain 75 cents or a dollar, big deal! After all, it is a job.

Good luck, Mr. Segraves, but the new will soon wear off, and you will have to put on an apron and walk the floors and "fill" the lady's grocery list yourself.

Gather around group, for you are about to witness one of the most important and appreciated business endeavors in our fair city. We stand before one of the three Greek Cafes that Fitzgerald boasts of. The tireless operator-owner is Nick Pope, his family working by his side. (Nick Pope owned the Liberty Cafe at 216 E. Pine in 1937. Later, the cafe moved to 123 S. Sherman St., according to the 1950 City Directory.)

I don't know when this fellow sleeps. He is at his grill about 20 hours a day. Rain or shine, heat or freeze, Nick Pope was on the job, feeding hungry people.

I had to meet a train at 3 a.m., and as I waited for the newspapers to come from Atlanta on the morning train, no cars were on the street to speak of. In the darkness, I could see headlights coming down the street, and I could safely say, "Well, it won't be long before the train comes 'sailing in.'" Sure enough, the faithful old "silver streak" black Pontiac automobile, showing its age and two or three hundred thousand miles rolled under the streetlight. You guessed it. Nick Pope was headed to fire up his grill one more morning. Maybe we should erect a statue to him, with the other "greats" who made this city what it is. May his grill never go cold, and that old Pontiac car never fail to fire off in the stillness of the wee hours.

My father told me as a wee lad that he came to the Colony City in 1910, and not long after, he and Nick were initiated in the Masonic Order. Nick didn't speak much, but he could give you a look that left little doubt how he felt about a subject. He didn't smile much either, but his old heart was as big as all of Texas and maybe a bit of Oklahoma.

Let me at this point give a bit of advice—act right and don't go shooting off your mouth or you will probably go sailing out those folding glass doors that open right on the sidewalk—the well-worn sidewalk—landing on your ear. Nick has zero tolerance for hell-raising in his cafe. (Paul describes Nick's place as having accordion glass doors. "When they were open, the doors were open. There was no front door. You just walked in." Across the front, he says, there was a display of fruit, bananas, oranges and apples, and a fish box full of ice, with scales hanging down for use in weighing the fish. All the cooking was done behind the counter, in full view of the customers who sat at the counter. "They had a nice marble counter, with little enameled white stools that turned around." Paul says they "mopped and scrubbed the floor all the time. They were cluttered, but they were not dirty." There were creaking ceiling fans overhead and, in the back, a large exhaust fan sucked air through to keep flies out. Behind the bar, there were rows of bottled wine, which it was legal to sell then. Beer was served on the countertop in tall-necked brown bottles—Schlitz and Silver Fox, the latter a brand Paul says he's never seen anywhere else. In those days, people didn't get beer to go.

The cafe was famous for three things, Paul says—its good, hearty breakfasts of bacon, eggs and coffee, the Irish stew Nick cooked up for lunch and served with oyster crackers, the oyster stew he made with milk and cream and fried mullet, which could be served on a sandwich or as a lunch plate, in whatever amount the customer desired. "It was good food. Nick himself did most of the cooking." Many people came in early in the morning and late at night, because the cafe was open when nothing else was.)

Nick has a little desk in the rear of the cafe. I was a

stamp collector in the pre-war days and I sometimes got up the nerve to ask him if he had any stamps on the letters he received from the old country, Greece. He would say not a word, but wipe his hands on his white apron, stick his lips out and hand them to me. I would swell up, I was so proud of them.

As I got older, I would carefully save old newspapers, tie them in bundles that would fit in my bicycle basket and pedal through the streets or alleys to Nick's cafe. I would have to wait until he finished his last order, then he would silently inspect them, weigh the bundle on his fish scales, walk to the cash register, punch the "no sale" key and pay me a penny a pound for them. He used them to wrap fish. From this, I would have enough cash to go to the picture show and get a Baby Ruth candy bar. I also dreamed of the day that I could walk in off the sidewalk, remove my hat, order a fried mullet sandwich and a frosty cold bottle of Schlitz beer and hear "Old Nick" say the only words I ever heard him say: "Coming right up!" Then see him or Spiro Samaltinos slide them down that spotless marble counter.

I must tell you, he believes in family closeness, especially when the floor needs mopping or the grill needs cleaning. If school, which he believes in, wasn't in session his two older sons, George and Paul "Puddy," manned the mop, which they had learned to do when they were knee-high to a grasshopper. Mrs. Pope is also a tireless worker, bless her Irish heart, and is a friend to all, especially the neighborhood kids who always hang around the home place on West Central Avenue at supper time. She takes a deep breath as she looks at all the little faces round the dinner table and exclaims, "All of these kids just can't be mine!" Not anyone ever leaves hungry that I know of.

The movie serial, "Our Gang," could have selected a whole new cast at her house.

'"Shut up, old story teller. We have one other place

to see up the street."

All right, folks, but before we depart, I must say, everybody passes through these folding doors—workmen, salesmen, pool sharks, no-accounts, policemen, city fathers, taxi drivers, loan sharks, brick masons, used car salesmen, railroad crews, road contractors, merchants, maybe even preachers, mostly men, all hungry or thirsty.

That bunch of bananas, ice box of fresh fish (speckled trout, croakers, mullet, redfish, catfish) right on the sidewalk, white aprons, little stools at the counter, ceiling fans that stir the steamy air, the laughter of men who have probably had one Silver Fox beer too many or a joke that only men would find funny—life on the half shell.

We must go, see you later!

Mr. Jake Tatel has a dry goods store on one side of the Greek Cafe. Lawrence Portier has a barber shop on the other side. Nothing vacant around here. Mr. Tatel can fit anyone. He may have been a tailor, I don't know, but he knows his suits and pants. He has a smile and handshake for any passer by, bar none. His wife is noted around town as a wonderful cook and is in great demand on the Cafe Circuit. Their son Bill is a very popular young man. His sister Rita was also a very popular student at old Fitz-High. New York City has its garment district and so does Fitzgerald. With the exception of one more cafe, up on the alley, clothing or dry goods are the overwhelming businesses. One large store, the Fair Store, established by Alex Kruger, is managed by his charming son, Buddy, and his wife, Rosalie. Mr. Moore, Mr. Jim Young and several lady clerks stay busy waiting on customers trying to dress their families on a modest budget. It's a busy place on Saturdays.

The other storefronts are smaller shops run by Jewish merchants, with a few exceptions. Eli Grigsby is one. He has a popular store featuring work clothes and shoes, kind of a mom-and-pop business. I say that because

Mrs. Grigsby and their son stay at the door, greeting any passing shopper. Great salesmen, these people.

Now let's visit Mr. Sam Abram and his wife at another dry goods outlet offering, maybe, higher priced goods. Their claim to fame is their brilliant sons, among whom is Morris Abram, a scholar and author who is headed to the top, far beyond these crowded sidewalks. Go get 'em, Morris. Put Fitzgerald on the map.

Next among our clothing merchants is Martin Gottlieb, gentleman if one ever lived. He might even be a candidate for our "hall of fame" and get a statue in the Central Avenue park. A poor, itinerant Jewish tailor by trade, who was passing through the booming Colony early on, he had everything he owned on his back. He started working for an established merchant, altering suits and pants for prominent men. His work impressed his customers and even his employers, who encouraged him to stay on and helped him set up a tailor shop here on E. Pine Street.

It wasn't long until his suits were worn by doctors, lawyers, politicians, why even old Gene Talmadge had a handmade suit over those famous red suspenders, all made by the patient, skillful fingers of Martin Gottlieb and his young apprentice, a gentile boy, Ed Castleberry, whom he groomed into a business partner. Alec White is their assistant. Here they are, with tape measures hung around their necks. Top of the line, fellows. I only hope that someday my "pattern" will be in your file.

From our vantage point here at the middle of the 200-block of E. Pine Street, looking across at the south side of the street, I see a thriving auto parts business, recently opened by some local young men, Charles Steed, Bill Barr, Dewey Smith and Walt Tucker. There seems to be no end to the need for auto parts.

Next door, Jimmie and Frances Hiers have opened a nice jewelry store, a great addition to the lineup. They are the official watch checkers for the railroad. All the transportation employees, engineers, conductors, firemen and flag men, must have their watches inspected monthly, as their lives depend on the time of day or night. Seldom is there a time that there is not a crew member pulling out a gold pocket watch, mostly a 21-jewel Hamilton, with good-natured Jimmie Hiers comparing it to the big "official" clock on the wall above him. The employee then signs the register. "See you next month, ol' pal," Jimmie always says. (This electric clock was tied into the railroad's time-keeping system and kept up to the minute in accuracy. The railroad business, and many lives, depended on all the workers being synchronized.)

Frances sells many an engagement ring to young men in love. Wylene Vaughn adds much charm as a sales lady. The two know every silver, china and crystal pattern that young brides have selected. It's always a pleasure to step into Hiers Jewelry Store.

Before we go on, ever westward, there is no better time to point out a few people who make this block their home. Oh, they are not homeless, or unhappy, or bums. They just love this sidewalk, and it loves them.

I believe I see Will Cleveland's taxi cab here in front of the second Greek Cafe that Fitzgerald boasts, City Fruit and Lunch Room, owner-manager Bill Pope and his beautiful wife, Mary.

Will Cleveland has a "vintage" Ford two-seater with a convertible top and four doors, around a 1932 year model. Will himself has been around since Colony days, and must have several million miles on him. Arthritis has left him bent in a crescent, but it doesn't slow him down. He has a taxi driver's cap on and can take you to Cordele if you need to go.

Charlie Simpson is busy hauling people about. Don't overlook Cuff Lott and his Blue Bird Cabs—love that name. Jake Stone drives when he feels like it. Isom

Hungate helps out also. These boys know every street and alley in urban and rural Ben Hill County and probably could go through them blindfolded.

The Liles brothers have a cab stand around the corner, Yellow Cab. They have telephones, but these old boys just sit and wait.

The black community also has cab drivers. Henry Stickney, a retired railroad brake man, drives a battered old cab, taking women who cook and clean all over town. Watch out for Henry and "Mud Cat" as they deliver their fares at about 7 a.m.

I see the old fellow who comes to town every weekend in his well kept Model T Ford, parks it at the corner, raises the trunk or "cooter hull" and stands up a large velvet-covered display board with rows of costume jewelry. Nice stuff, too. He sits beside it in a straight chair, open for business. (A "cooter hull" is an old name for the trunk in the South, comparing the trunk to a turtle's shell.)

Here comes a short black man wearing a battered old felt hat, with kitchen matches stuck in the band, and a pair of knee-high rubber boots. He is pushing a rubber-tired push cart with a 55-gallon steel barrel mounted between the wheels, a rack on both sides, containing a scoop shovel, a seed fork and a large brush broom. He usually has a stub of a cigar clenched in his teeth. We boys named him Rich Rush. He works hard at his job as street sweeper. He is never idle, and the sidewalks and brick streets are unblemished, even with quite a few mules and horses still pulling wagons and frequent parades. How "Rich" keeps the whole uptown clean, I don't know. Maybe he deserves a statue in the park also.

Down the alley, if you look closely, you may see another well-known black man sitting in a small one-horse wagon. The wagon is so rickety and the wheels wobble so badly, you might wonder if it will make it home. This is "Slop" Jackson and the barrel behind his seat is filled with swill, or slops, that the cafe operators and cooks save for him. He is one of the great pork producers in this area. His hogs squeal and snort as he approaches their pens. Jackson's hogs are highly esteemed.

Old Uncle Dan, another slop collector, lives over by the railroad tracks, but he has no mules and wagon. He patrols the alleys with a wheel barrow and two five-gallon lard cans. He is a small operator, but he is the best natured of the three operators, and we boys loved to sit around his cabin and hear his tales. I don't think this group will be around long.

Sam Chester, a prosperous black merchant, respected by all, doesn't have a business along here. His store is east of here, on Monitor Drive. Sam has a great wit and plenty of money. No tour would be thorough, if Sam wasn't mentioned. His sense of humor, and a dialect of his very own and his pure old wisdom must be remembered.

Strolling the street along this section is "Little John," his guitar strumming away as he sings some plaintive love song. A tin cup wired on the end clinks as a coin drops in. (Paul says that Little John's cup was wired to the end of his guitar so that he could "point" it at the people he played for.)

The aroma of Nick Pope's rich Irish stew floats by. It never fails to draw all the street people from their lair. I see Bob Littlefield, Horace Buckalew, Wiggly Smith on his crutches. John Padgett just passed. Spence Scruggs. Hoot Gibson. Old deaf Charlie Myrick, Milton "Big Hat" Rathburn, Paul Portier, Red Rawlins, the police force with their wide awake chief, Gordon Roberts, Tom Greer, Jehu Fletcher, the cattle baron of nearby Irwin County and a good farmer. Could that be Cowboy Smith, the millionaire bridge builder? George Talbot, the elite of the railroad engineers, Arthur Smith, talking to himself, even Jimmie Hiers. Hey, Jimmie, won't you give me your rendition of "Sweet Adeline"? "Dutch" Kilburn, the German sign painter who paints murals on walls. Dip deep, Nick Pope, these boys want a little meat.

Early one Saturday morning before Pine Street woke up, I saw Joe Rigdon, a hardworking tank shed foreman at the railroad shops, parking the family sedan by the dawn's early light in one of the best parking spaces, roll the windows up and walk home ten blocks away. Joe didn't have car trouble, he just wanted the car in a good position so that he and his good wife, Lula, and their three boys and one girl, would have a place to sit and watch the "show" that afternoon, then drive home after dark. And he wasn't the only one to do such.

My, my, boys. If the good lord had built me a fence around a four-block area hereabout and a ticket booth, a brass band with musicians in moth-eaten uniforms, a big roll of tickets selling at ten cents each, I would by now be a millionaire, like Mr. P.T. Barnum, the circus king. I would not have needed a tent or had to pay clowns or any performers, no monkeys or jackasses, all of which would have paid a thin dime just to enter. Oh well, you'll just have to be here next Saturday evening. The show is on the town, but come early, friend, because you may not be able to find a good parking place!

Back to the real world, come to order, and look across the street. There, soaring to three brick stories is the aging lady of a hotel, the once-elegant Aldine, renamed the Jeff Davis Hotel, named in the good spirit of the Yank-Reb Colony City, as Jeff Davis was the president of the Confederate States of America, now defunct. This once popular hotel was managed by Mr. Nat Moore.

Ol' Jeff was captured near here while being pursued by two groups of Yankee cavalrymen trying to surround his camp. One group of Yanks mistook the other group, and they had a terrific battle amongst themselves, but finally became oriented and captured Jeff Davis and his group.

I am no history professor, but the old hotel is about to surrender also, much as its namesake, but this time the captors aren't on horseback. It is simply progress—and a leaking roof. It is to be renovated and we hear that the Dixieland 5 & 10 Cent Store is moving here, managed by a young man named Felton Watson.

Don't be surprised if you see a ghost or two about, Felton, as some of the best "performers" have rested their weary heads on the snow-white pillows in the bedrooms above your Dixieland store.

Let me tell you about one of my favorite guests—a permanent guest, as he made his home in a suite of rooms that he had leased. He had his parlor, his office, his trophy room, his gun collection, pool table, bar, guest rooms, etc., here.   He was H.G. Smith, a civil engineer, bridge contractor and sportsman. The world was his playground. He dressed in tailored jackets, a big man, you might even say he was handsome. His riding pants were tucked into riding boots, shined to perfection, and he wore a ten-gallon, pearl gray Stetson hat.   He could have been mistaken for Ernest Hemingway or Jack London. Along the way, he had acquired the appropriate nickname, Cowboy Smith. He was, I thought, a dead ringer for Tom Mix. He loved guns and had a vast collection of Smith and Wesson pistols and Winchester rifles.   He had been on hunting expeditions to Alaska and the West. His trophy room was loaded with moose heads, their antlers spread out like umbrellas, mountain goats ready to leap high cliffs, Kodiak brown bears ready to charge, eagles soaring, all upstairs over the lobby and cafe run by waitress Izola Mangum. He was a real gentleman, of a bygone era. It was said that he had an uncanny knack for always voting for the winning governor of this state. All I am sure of is that his Smith Construction Co. is building a lot of bridges.

I think he also just enjoyed E. Pine Street and the Greek restaurants. He would take his game and fish across

Pine Street to Nick or Bill Pope, to get them to prepare it for him and, sometimes, him and his guests. You might even see Gov. Ed Rivers or the state transportation representative enjoying his hospitality. Many business deals were sealed under the blinking, half-burned-out neon sign that tried to flash "Jeff Davis Hotel." A contract signed at the Jeff Davis is just as valid as one signed at the Waldorf Astoria Hotel under the glittering lights of Times Square in far off New York City.

(According to the 1937 and 1950 city directories, Cowboy Smith had an office on the fourth floor of the Garbutt-Donovan Building. In later years, O.W. Fletcher owned the Jeff Davis Hotel and remodeled it, and Cowboy Smith moved his office, and his trophies, across the street to the old Greek cafe building. He moved to the Lee-Grant Hotel and, as his health began to fail, he employed a long-time orderly at Ben Hill County Hospital to drive for him and dress him. Paul notes that the hospital, where he was born, was founded by Dr. D.B. Ware and Dr. R.M. Ware. After Cowboy Smith's move to the Lee-Grant, Paul says, "His old friends dropped in and visited him. He was still full of spirit. I often saw men who were legends in their own times, some of them in wheelchairs, with him. They spun yarns of past days and had a toddy with him. He was a hard act to follow.")

Leaving the old hotel behind, Royce Williams's billiard parlor is next. Business men drop in to "fram" a few games and get the latest low down news. You know men don't gossip.

Next door, a new business is open. The Yancey brothers, Wimp and Scooter, hometown boys who managed to return from World War II, have opened the Firestone Store, offering sporting and automotive goods that were unobtainable during the war years. Mac Anderson is helping them. Good luck, fellows. I have recently bought an outboard motor from them. (Rosemary, daughter of Wimp Yancey, says her father managed the Champion Store, commonly called the Firestone Store, and Benny Anderson owned it.)

Rogers Food Store is next, one of the new trend of supermarkets.

A substantial, brick building sits squarely on the prime-located corner of Grant and Pine street, kind of the crossroads of the business district. For years Mr. Renfro Walker and his helper, Nelson Walker, has operated the Stewart-Mitchell Hardware Store. He has moved to a new building around the corner, with his own store, Walker Hardware. (Paul says Stewart-Mitchell was part of a chain of hardware stores. When it moved from its 201 E. Pine St. location, it went into the S. Grant Street building. John Hageman, who also worked for Renfro Walker after he came back from the war, says that in those days hardware stores didn't just sell parts to do-it-yourselfers. He and Nelson worked a lot of hard, dirty jobs, installing flues in tobacco barns, putting in well pumps and more.)

A newcomer has opened a jewelry store with the catchy name the Jolly Jeweler. Herbert Moore is his name and he is a crackerjack watch repairman and a great addition to the uptown merchants. His wife, Monteen, works with him. He has a novel sign outside along Grant Street—twelve yellow plastic dish pans, with electric bulbs mounted inside, with one letter on the bottom of each one, spelling out the name of the business. They look OK during the day, but come alive at night when he switches the lights on. Some display.

He has a smile that beams, day or night! Monteen's red hair is also highly visible. Nice people!

The jewelry business seems to be thriving here in downtown Fitzgerald, as there are two or three more just up the street. I suppose wedding rings are hot on the market on account of so many soldier boys returning home to their sweethearts. Marriage and home seem to be on the young people's minds. Nothing wrong with that, and diamonds don't grow on trees, you know.

Wait up there, group, I have overlooked an outstanding street character and here he comes, pushing a worn-out lawn mower, almost as worn out as he has become. His name is Drew Hill, a black man. In his young days, he was about the strongest man I knew, he and Leroy Bowen. Leroy worked at the Seaboard Railroad Depot, and Drew was a delivery man for the cotton mill, along with Clint Giddens. Both were faithful servants and took great pride in their strength, demonstrating it on occasion. Both could pick up and carry a 500-lb. bale of cotton on their backs, bodies bulging with glistening muscle that rippled beneath their skin. Both were happy and courteous—and woe be to anyone who would mistreat either one.

Now the Fourth of July was a big day, in the square where Central and Main street cross. A boxing ring of sorts was erected and a match was made. Now don't think Drew Hill wasn't a world-class fighter. LeRoy Bowen wasn't far behind, although he wasn't as fast as Drew. Drew was open to all challengers and usually won the match, hands down, but every year, old LeRoy would climb into the ring and shake gloved hands with Drew. Morgan Bryant would be referee. The bell would ring. LeRoy would stand flat-footed and Drew would "dance" around LeRoy, knowing that he could drive him in the ground like a stake. The crowd would shout and lay bets. Finally LeRoy would tire and Drew would land a devastating blow on LeRoy and win the bout.

Now, my friends, Joe Louis was world champ, but he never met Drew Hill. Who knows, old Drew might have put that haymaker on old famous Joe and Morgan Bryant in his striped shirt and his cauliflower ears would have been slowly counting to ten over his sound asleep body.

Nowadays, LeRoy has gone to his reward and Drew

mows a few lawns around town. His teeth are gone and his frame is gaunt and bent, but his smile still spreads across his wrinkled face when I holler, "Get him, Champ."

A while back, an electric wire was blown down and Drew's great strength wasn't a match for the surge of electricity that went through his old body. He lived, but lost an arm. Here he comes, pushing that wobbly old mower with one hand. He still isn't down for the count.

Joe Louis and LeRoy Bowen must look down on him. Old Drew Hill is over the hill, but he doesn't know it. That spirit is what made this Colony City a success.

Come on, my footsore sightseers, I have tarried long enough. Let's wait for a green light and cross Grant Street and turn to the left before the well-worn marble steps of the old First National Bank building. The bank went broke in the Depression in 1929. It still is a splendid old landmark building. I wish I could have known the master brick mason who laid the ornate brick pattern that adorns the cornice and eaves of the two-story edifice. Time has only mellowed the marble steps at the front. Many steps of anxious customers have smoothed this marble—and many loafers, sitting on them since the old girl has been vacant. The steps kind of make a grandstand for watching the "parade" each Saturday.

Not to mention the police officer, looking the crowd over. You understand, for many years the police station was quartered in the basement of this bank building. The steps that descend to the basement are steep and enclosed by a stout cast-iron pipe bannister that serves to keep pedestrians on the Grant Street side of the building from "dropping in" on the chief and his trusty force. Outside is the call box—a red metal box, it is the "911" of 1946. When the phone inside rings, a policeman comes running to unlock the box and answer the emergency call.

There is no yard. The building is surrounded by sidewalk. A big yellow sign warns "No parking. Police."

The chief's patrol car and the black maria to haul offenders to jail are parked outside, and the speed cop's souped up Ford car with the siren mounted on the front fender waits to scratch off, sirens wailing, Milton Findley crouched behind the wheel.

When the entire force was assembled, three of Fitzgerald's finest, the room was filled to capacity. The dog catcher had to sit on the steps.

Late at night some teenage boys would lob a firecracker down these forbidding steps and run like crazy. Night officer Joe Fussell, who liked to lean back in his swivel chair and take a nap after midnight, would turn over trying to catch the culprits and would live up to the force's motto, "Always wide awake."

Wait a minute, folks. I am not through with this historic old girl. Surely if Fitzgerald ever has a historic register, she will be right up at the top. I only wish she could talk, with these old marble steps and carefully placed bricks with the ornate scroll stating in bold letters "BANK" over the mission oak double doors. She could tell about the investors' dreams, workmen who cashed their hard-earned checks, loans that sent promising students to college or handsome young bankers and young women, dressed in the latest fashions, floor sweepers and dust women. The vanished savings of frugal people just trying to get by. Then one morning the bank failed to open, and the shades were drawn, showing the solemn word "closed" and it stayed closed. A crowd of angry, disgruntled people gathered, holding tear-stained deposit books and worthless stocks and bonds—the panic of 1929 had fallen, just as those door blinds had, during the night. I understand the president and some other bank officials caught the midnight passenger train for points unknown. Have a good trip, boys, but don't come back soon. What have you got in those long black suitcases? Surely you don't own that many suits?

Oh well, if only this beautiful, now vacant, building could talk, she could do a much better job than I can, for I was just a lad sitting on my father's drooped shoulder. Yes, Fitzgerald has a grapevine for inside information before the Herald or Leader breaks the news. The grapevine has it that a prominent businessman and 10 investors are going to buy this building and open a bank. Better get on your toes, National Bank. Hope you can handle some competition.

The town is booming, people have jobs and want to spend their money on cars and homes, now that the war is over and the materials are available.

One of our most capable and civic-minded citizens, Capt. Jack Dorminy, has an office in the rear, or Grant street, entrance to this old bank building (the original First National Bank building) and his bookkeeper, Mrs. Meeks, is a valued employee. Fitzgerald is fortunate to have men like him. He is a "captain" for real, his very appearance gives people confidence. He is truly a captain of industry and business.

Eugene Strickland, Capt. Jack's son-in-law and son of old-time Police Chief Strickland, has his insurance office here. He is very popular and has a large clientele. See you, Gene!

Up Grant Street is the office of another "captain" who goes by the name of Phillip Halperin, our anchor man of the Jewish merchants who have contributed so much to the economy of this fair city. His secretary and bookkeeper is Mrs. Harris. She knows those books.

Change is in motion hereabouts. These old storefronts are being remodeled. Every day a new business or service appears on the streets we all love. Mr. Bailey's old bicycle repair shop is being remodeled. He is aging, I reckon. Lyman Brewer will have to find another job. Mr. Bailey has repaired many a bicycle, over a number of years, and is going to have a shop in his backyard at home. Keep 'em rolling, Mr. Bailey. (Jefferson Bailey lived at 211 E. Jessamine. After he closed his shop at 209 S. Grant, he continued to repair bikes at his home until he died, Paul says.)

As we move south on the 200-block of Grant Street, a lineup of service shops appear. Coot Norris, a veteran barber, has his own small shop here. He has cut my hair since the 1930s when he had to put a board across the arm rest of the large barber chair with the hand lever on the side to adjust the height to accommodate each individual customer. The going price for a boy's haircut was 25 cents, but my mom made me walk farther, to Coot's shop, because he charged only 20 cents. At that time, a nickel looked as large as a manhole cover.

Coot has three chairs, I think. Eddie Hilton is on the second chair and Walt Owens on the third. Coot has a man's face wrapped in a hot towel, the chair cranked back to where the man is lying flat out and Coot is honing his straight razor on a shiny leather strop to sharpen it to perfection.

Dow Brown, one of Fitzgerald's beloved characters, just walked in. As always, he is dapper looking in a nice suit of clothes, white shirt and necktie and polished Florsheim shoes, his felt hat with the silk hat band set on his head at a jaunty angle. Now, Dow is talented in several fields, among which is song and dance, especially dance. He can do the "pigeon wing" buck dance. I reckon the only dance Dow can't do is ballet. He may give us a rendition any minute.

When the minstrel show Silas Green from New Orleans comes to Fitzgerald aboard their special train with its coaches that are painted green, and the tent is raised down on Mead Street, Dow Brown can give lessons to the professional dancers. He was born with rhythm in him.

His other talent is pharmacy. He is a chemist with shade-tree talent. He has a skin cancer remedy that is famous far and wide. People come to his home in limousines, horse and buggies, pickup trucks, bicycles, even wheelbarrows, for treatment. He won't disclose his formula. Doctors have tried to buy it, but he won't sell. I reckon that recipe will go to the grave with him. Truly one of old Fitzgerald's famed sons.

We could hang around the barber shop till noon. These shops draw characters like sugar does bees. Good day, Coot, and may your hand be steady.

Doris Pridgen with her red hair and brown eyes has a beauty shop along here. She has a noble project, to beautify the ladies of the Colony City. She and several other beauty operators work long hours doing their best to clip and curl hair, give permanents and facials. Now folks, I am trying to tell you about something I know very little about, as men are not permitted inside. The path to feminine beauty is not always flattering to the individual.

Oh, move on, storyteller and speak about something you might know a little about.

Doris, you may need to be a magician to help some of these girls instead of a mere beautician.

Look here, a new cafe has opened. The Yanceys, Wimp and his wife Dickey, have gone to much effort and expense to give Fitzgerald a new place to dine out. The catchy name is the Purple Duck. Now whoever heard of a purple duck? Things smell great here on the sidewalk. The kitchen opens right on the alley and a huge exhaust fan is blowing all the cooking aromas right down the street. Dickey's sister, Inez Archer, is a talented artist and has painted wall murals of ducks and barnyard animals all about the booths that line the wall. Walt Disney would hire her on the spot if he saw the animals parading around the dining room walls.

How was Fitzgerald blessed with so many talented citizens? Whatever the need is, someone will rise up and do a splendid job. No need to send off to New York or even Hollywood. We have their equal right among us here on these beloved sidewalks.

I have already mentioned Renfro Walker, the hardware merchant. We are passing his new, or rather, remodeled building. He has much more room and a nice glass front. Passers by can now window shop, a popular pastime during an evening or on a Sunday stroll uptown. You may see something you need to buy when you have a few frog skins in your pocket.

I remember buying a Winchester pump 16-gauge shotgun here, in 1943, during the war, when new guns were not on the market. Renfro had gotten them at an army surplus sale, from the Air Corps. The guns were used to teach aerial machine gunners on Flying Fortresses to shoot down German Messerschmitts over Europe. Now, wasn't I lucky? Paid $25 for it. I had the $25 thanks to Nick Pope buying newspapers to wrap fish and Ashley Downing for buying scrap iron and copper to help the war effort. Elie Vickers also bought bamboo fishing poles that I carefully trimmed for him. There were none coming from Japan. I could cut and trim 100 a day. He would pay me ten cents each for them. I could carry 25 at a time to Lake Beatrice, tied on either side of my bicycle. I don't remember where I sat, but I got them there OK. Then spent my money on a shotgun! I was in the 10th grade at good old Fitzgerald High School. Yes, I was part of the sidewalk scene, right along here.

(Paul says that Ashley Downing had a junkyard beside the railroad track on N. Grant Street. A black man named Hollis weighed the scrap metal that was bought in and Virginia Hunter paid out the money for it. Dowling bought anything made of metal and bought radiators and batteries for their copper and lead. Copper was especially valuable during the war years, Paul says. But prior to that, he says, scrap iron was shipped from here to Savannah, where it was put on board ships bound for Yokohama,

Japan. People used to say that the Japanese shot it back at us during the war, Paul says.)

Ball's Bakery is next. Barney Ball is an independent baker who operates this hometown enterprise. He doesn't have to advertise. The aroma that drifts down the street is all that is needed. He has a small white panel truck, with a large red spot painted on the side, with the words "Ball's Bakery" below. His light bread is ten cents a loaf, a nickel for day-old. I reckon you know which age bread we ate at home. His cinnamon buns are out of this world.

He never gave any of us boys a bun, but two beautiful cheerleaders later admitted that "Ol' Barn" had presented one of his famous buns to each of them. On another day they said they had to walk past three times before they could get him to notice them outside his shop. Oh well, that's the breaks. Everyone can't be beautiful, but everyone gets hungry. (Mr. Ball's wife, Mona, worked in the bakery with him.)

Everyone has about forgotten that Fitzgerald had a Yank-Reb beginning. A few of the Northern citizens are around still. Ed Whitman has a tinsmith shop along here. He is about retired, as he is almost 90 years old, but he still hammers around in his old shop. He made most of the gutters and kitchen table tops in town. (Maurice E. Whitman's shop was located at 223 S. Grant St. in 1937.)

Burns Cleaners is next, a dry cleaning business of many years, and clothes that have been carefully cleaned and hung in cellophane and paper bags with a ticket clipped to the shoulder wait for their owners to call for them.

People take good care of their "Sunday go to meeting" clothes, as they must last for years. Those war years were a rut on everybody—shortages, rationing, low wages, etc., but things are looking better nowadays.

Come on, old man, we have a ways to go yet, and the day is growing old like you.

Well, if you are waiting on me, you are "backing up."

Melvin and Nora Fletcher, along with their beautiful young daughter, Martha, are hometown folks and own a delightful china shop here at the corner of Magnolia and Grant street. They live upstairs over the store. This is kind of the end of the downtown business district.

Can't brag on the shop and its proprietors enough. Some of the nicest gifts are from this shop. Everyone loves to browse around. (Later the Fletchers opened Melnor Manufacturing on E. Central, taking the business name from their first names.)

A small space on the corner, just a nook to be sure, is a lunch wagon. It really isn't a wagon, but it is no larger. Just a lunch counter and a grill. A smiling, slender young man, in a white jacket and cook's white "top hat" runs the place. He is Chuck. He just drifted into town and has won everyone's hearts in a few years. He runs it by himself and opens early and closes late-late. Frieda Graham Jacobson and her husband own the business but are Chuck's silent partners. (The 1950 City Directory identifies the proprietor of the Snack Shack as Charles S. Jacobson, Frieda's husband.)

A dozen people are a crowd here. A big fan roars away at the end. On a cold winter's night, after the movies on Sunday night, you and your date—to you the most beautiful girl in the world—could arrive on your trusty Cushman scooter and sit at the counter and order a waffle with syrup and a steaming cup of hot chocolate with a marshmallow floating on top. The Rock-Ola juke box plays "Kiss me once, kiss me twice, kiss me once again, it's been a long, long time." Go on, lover boy, give ol' Chuck one of your hard-earned dollar bills, bundle Miss Hollywood up good, seat her on the buddy seat, kick that kick starter and putt off down the dark street. Hope her mama and dad aren't sitting up waiting. On her return, you may not even get a good night kiss. Your cash assets probably aren't but fifteen cents—it won't even jingle in your pocket—but it will buy enough gasoline to last till next weekend, with luck.

Ol' Chuck exhausts enough greasy smoke and fumes from that grill till, for years to come, paint won't stick to that brick wall behind it.

Robert Bruce Liles has a Yellow Cab stand on the vacant lot around the corner on Magnolia, but we kids just didn't have the fare. "Shine on harvest moon"—maybe that is why all those jewelry stores are doing such a land office business.

Just stand here on the corner and look across Magnolia street and you shall see the prestige auto business, the Buick dealership of Monroe Fletcher, a dapper, middle-aged bachelor, a native of Irwin County. He dresses well. You might say he is a fashion plate. His customers come from far and wide to buy Buick automobiles from him. He has a shop behind his show room, with a competent staff of mechanics, Dewey Smith Sr. and Emitt Vickers, assisted by faithful helper, Reese Moton.

Monroe has a diamond ring upon his well-manicured finger, nearly as large as a 75-cent piece of ice, and it sparkles a lot more. He is seldom without a 25-cent King Edward cigar, seldom lit. His walking cane has a gold handle and his barber shaves him every day. He has a handkerchief with a large "F" monogrammed on it folded properly in his breast pocket and a shirt as white as the snows of Kilimanjaro, with gold cufflinks at his wrist.

He can sell a car to the governor, quite a gentleman, but no lady has been able to steer him to the altar, and he has sold many a rich widow a fine automobile, and they love him. His younger brother, "Doc" Fletcher, is never far away, although he looks about like the rest of us guys.

Look both ways and let's cross Grant Street to the east side. Here, we are standing in front of the large brick

Coca-Cola bottling plant, owned by the now deceased J. Benton. It is managed by Clyde Daniel and operated by Ed Walker. It, like the Dr. Pepper plant, has a conveyor belt carrying freshly bottled Coca-Cola's past the lady inspector. Mrs. George Ellis, sitting in her high chair, visually inspects every famous bottle as it passes her, either to be put in yellow cypress wood crates and loaded onto a truck by Simmie. He and the long-time route man, Rufus Pate, will now go off to stores, rural and urban with the tinkling glass bottles filled once more with the dark liquid that is famous, world wide. People come and buy them by the crate. You bring a crate full of empty bottles and get a full one. The drink costs only a nickel, if you drink it where it is sold. You have to pay a two- to five-cent deposit if you take the bottle with you. Another business opportunity for children and anybody else is collecting empty Coke bottles and taking them back to the plant to collect the deposit.

One well-known millionaire who has to walk for his health is rumored to have caches all over town for the bottles he collects on his walks. Next day he retrieves his collection for the refund.

Several outlying stores make a business of brokering bottles, paying one cent less than the plant. Brooks Davis, over by the radio station, has 10,000 bottles on hand and is the undisputed king of the brokers. Some day the bottles will be plastic, throw-away bottles. What will children and millionaires do for a little pocket change?

But we are not on this tour to decide the future of the Coca-Cola Company. They have a board of directors to do that.

The Ford Motor Company lies behind me and the home office, not Ford Motor, but the business holdings of Bennie Anderson, a transplant.

He could care less about whether he is northern or southern. He is here in Fitzgerald because he saw a business opportunity in this fledgling city. The Yankees who came were poor and tired of ice and snow, but they had the necessities of life. Now, the Georgia "crackers" who were native hereabout were hard put to make a living on pine forest and worn-out, eroded cotton land. There were the poor and the very poor. They needed a market for their peanuts, corn, cotton, pine tar and livestock. Mr. B.I. Anderson and several others developed these markets that we have now. He also made it possible for these hard scrabble Southerners to buy a Model A Ford pickup truck and keep it clicking. Mr. Spell was his head bookkeeper. Dewitt Leverett was his parts manager, James Ray, head mechanic, and ever likable Chester Foster his head salesman. Damon Roberts is also a salesman here and Mr. Jones works at the Ford place, too. Yes, Fitzgerald Ford Company was vital in the development of this town and county of Ben Hill. There is no telling how many checks the Dixie Peanut Company handed out to local farmers.

Rex McEwen (books), Jake Miller (shelling plant) and Mr. Cherry (kept machinery working) run Mr. Anderson's peanut warehouse and shelling plant. Mr. McEwen would let me dig fish bait worms under the scales. The peanuts that fell under the scales made a great bait bed.

I expect Dixie shipped 100 railroad boxcars of peanuts all over America and abroad. The old song says, "When I was single, my pockets did jingle." Mr. Anderson, like several other successful businessmen in town, is single and he lives a very austere, plain lifestyle.

I hate to be in a hurry, but time flies and we have lingered too much already. I can smell those chopped onions that Wiley Floyd scatters on his grill when the hamburger business gets slow. We will follow our noses back up to the traffic light at the all-important corner of Pine and Grant streets. As the light turns green, let's cross over and look up at the only "skyscraper" Fitzgerald can boast, commonly known simply as the Five-Story Building.

I've read that it is properly known as the Garbutt-Donovan Building.   Nobody here on the sidewalk would know where you were talking about if you called it that.   They'd say, "Why didn't you call it the Five-Story Building?"

Well, there it is in all its glory.   How did a bunch of colonists build such a grand brick building?   It should be one of the Wonders of the Modern World.   Why, you can see clear to Lake Beatrice on a clear day if you ride the elevator to the fifth floor.   Why, just the creaking ride on the elevator, skillfully operated by Mr. Kratzer, one of our German immigrants to the Colony City, is quite an experience.

Mr. Kratzer must have been born with that long cigar that hangs limply from his lips as he concentrates on the floor numbers that flash by. (Paul says that Mr. Kratzer sat in a straight chair and when anyone came in, he went to the elevator and slammed open its iron "birdcage" gate. "You would go in and tell him what floor you wanted to go to. He had a throttle, a big lever, and he'd pull it to set it in motion."   As Paul remembers it, passengers could see the long cables as the car ascended and descended. Sometimes, Paul says, the floor of the car wouldn't line up properly with the floor outside when the doors opened and Mr. Kratzer would have to keep pulling his lever to get it right.)

Wiley Floyd has a lunch counter under the stair well. No tables, just a counter and a grill. His hamburgers are famous and the ladies who serve you smile and know just how you want your burger.   June Gibbs and Alice Freeman are standbys. Wiley has his white apron on and is busy turning hamburger patties.   Great people.   It just wouldn't be "uptown" without Floyd's. (One customer recalls that there were a few booths in Floyd's, on the other side of the entrance from the lunch counter.)

I will give you a rundown on the tenants of this large building—all of you can't get into the elevator.   Mr.

Kratzer might drop his cigar and we would exceed the posted load limit. So, let's start with Friedlander's clothing store, which occupies the entire ground, or first, floor. Entrances open onto Grant and Pine streets. We are back in the "garment district" after a detour. This is the largest of the clothing stores. High class clothes and shoes for men, women and children also. The business is owned by the Friedlander family of Moultrie. Mr. David C. and his son, Earl, are managers and salesmen. Mrs. Chester Brown is cashier. Mrs. Cliff Pickens and Mrs. Lea McNease, Mrs. Watson and several others are here to assist you in the proper selection of current styles.

Is that Vernie Horton putting up stock? Can't be. He is too young to be on the payroll. But it sure looks like him. Ladies clothing is sold on the mezzanine level upstairs. (Paul says that care was given to "dressing" the big plate glass windows to tempt passers by. All this care was wasted, however, when on the busiest day of the week, pedestrians perched on the window ledges, blocking the view of the wares displayed inside. To discourage this, the management placed boards with nails driven through them on the ledges, like a bed of nails.)

I would have to look at the bulletin board to give you the correct floor for the other tenants. Dr. Coffee has offices here. He is an eye, nose and throat doctor. I hear a young'un screaming as the good doctor holds down his tongue with a small wooden "paddle" and peers down his throat. He has a round mirror strapped to his forehead that is enough to scare the daylights out of any kid.

Don't forget Dr. W.E. Tuggle, the young dentist, and his assistant, Faustine Sheffield. Tuggle is a good dentist, but he sometimes fails to comprehend a patron's tolerance of pain, and he will always say, "See, I told you it wouldn't hurt." Kids heading for the dentist know they are going to "struggle with Tuggle."

A great hunter and fisherman, he loves the

Ocmulgee River and has one of the few outboard motors. It is an "off" brand, and he roars up the river if he can get the Water Witch motor cranked. I don't think he learned the language he describes his motor with at dental college!

Dr. Fred Daniels has a practice across the hall from Dr. Tuggle here in the Five Story Building. He is a popular chiropractor.   Dr. Daniels always makes a great appearance. He is a handsome man.

Mrs. Reason Paulk, a great lady, has a millinery shop on the same floor as the doctors. She makes ladies' hats and has been given the title of Mrs. "Hat" Paulk. I always stopped in her shop as a kid, to have a chat with her. She had no children, but all of us loved her and she could usually find a cookie to give us. Truly, one of the town's most honored ladies.

Emory Roberts has a finance company, with loans available. If you run a little "short" till payday, Emory or his son, Billy, will be glad to cross your palm with a small loan. Billy, don't you fall out that open window. That sidewalk is hard!

The state highway department has most of one upper floor. Ralph Sweat, resident engineer, comes down the elevator with his survey team and their instruments. I have already told you of H.G. "Cowboy" Smith. He at one time occupied a suite of offices on one floor. Onecia Starr and LaVern Hogan probably know more about the details of this operation than he does. I wouldn't doubt if the cowboy and several of his cronies aren't in Alaska, oiling up their rifles. Those big ol' brown bears had better find deep cave, or Mr. Smith will find the biggest one on Kodiak Island and send him all stuffed, glass eyes gleaming, to join his relatives right here in Fitzgerald, way up in the Five Story Building at the corner of Grant and Pine. Mr. Kratzer surely will drop his cigar when they load ol' papa bear on his creaking elevator.

Dr. Tuggle has an airplane. In his waiting room is

his "trophy," a wooden propellor now in a splintered condition, from one of his crashes, no doubt. I hope he has better luck keeping that zooming aircraft engine running than he does his Water Witch outboard motor.

Fitzgerald has more than its share of characters. When we get back on the street, I will tell you of a few.

When I was a lad, a crowd gathered on this corner, and it wasn't even Saturday. An old model limousine drove up Grant Street, which was also the Dixie Highway, Route #129, mainline to fabled Florida. The car parked and out stepped a young man, a black chauffeur and a beautiful peroxided blonde, whose lace-trimmed blouse was two sizes too small! She wore fishnet stockings with the seam going up the back.

The man was a circus daredevil, billing himself as the "Human Fly." He removed his shoes, flexed his slender body and proceeded to scale the bare brick face of the towering building, all five stories, then to sit on the eaves and salute the crowd far below. He came down on the elevator to be met by the cheering crowd of onlookers. His darling companion and his chauffeur passed the hat, and he bowed and smiled.

I expect Wiley Floyd took in about as much money as the Fly did, as he kept sprinkling his grill with chopped onions, and who could leave the sidewalk without one of his delicious hamburgers. That is, if they had fifteen cents.

Before we leave the Five Story Building, I want to tell you about another office here, run by Mr. George P. Morris. Mr. Morris is a relative of Mr. W. R. Bowen, a Southern owner of vast land holdings even before the Yankees came along. Mr. Morris is the agent for the farm and timber holdings of Mr. Bowen's estate, even the offices and stores we have just discussed.

Let's say farewell to this grand old building. May she dominate the skyline of our beloved city for many years. May the eaves of the old girl continue to furnish a safe haven and quiet roosting nooks for the flocks of pigeons that fly away at dawn to feed in the fields around town.   Mr. Morris hasn't collected any rent from these tenants. The pigeons just coo on. That fellow who just left in that old Cadillac, counting his change, the Human Fly, is the only person with the nerve and skill to visit them way up there on the roof.

Next door is another barber shop, with its candy-striped pole displayed. Mr. Bert Archer, Elmer's father, was clipping men's hair when I got shorn of my baby curls as my mother dabbed tears from her eyes. He is shaking out his "lap" sheet and calling "next," just as he will be doing when Mr. Jimmie Paulk, our undertaker, sends him on up to the Pearly Gates. A gentle, kind man, everyone thinks the world of him. I have told you enough of barber shops, but his is top of the line. He charges 25¢ a cut, but he brushes you off real god with his stout clothes brush. He also has a candy jar full of peppermint sticks to reward the children who sit on that hard bench and don't wiggle around or cry.   Mr. Archer has four chairs and two shoeshine chairs, and the shine boy can pop that shine rag like a rifle report, enough to scare the daylights out of a young'un. Big Boy Hall is a barber here.

My mom would say to me, "Now, son, don't be looking at pictures of those scantily clad movie stars in those magazines laying around on those waiting benches. Dorothy Lamour in a bathing suit. Jean Harlow in her nightgown and that wicked Bette Davis, Katherine Hepburn playing around with old Spencer Tracy. He ought to be horse-whipped, not to mention Clark Gable and his dirty mouth ("Frankly, my dear . . ."). It ought to be washed out with Octagon soap." She liked Nelson Eddy and Jeanette MacDonald, Charles Boyer and Leslie Howard. I like Burt Lancaster and Gregory Peck, not to mention Hoot Gibson and Tom Mix. Gene Autry sang too much.

Oh well, Fitzgerald has its actors also. The dry goods store next door is owned and operated by our Jewish friend from Lithuania, Abe Kruger. He does a great job manning his store, but he should have been out in Hollywood, Calif. The Marx Brothers were beginners beside him. He is Abe Kruger, never short of wit and humor.

He can call everyone by name, Miss Marjory Owen keeps books for him and Miss Alice Boles, whom I have mentioned before, is his clerk. His daughter Evelyn has beautiful blue eyes. He has another daughter, my classmate, named Adolphia. Abe's only son, Reuben, has a shoe store next door. Reuben's wife, Connie, is a jewel and Alma McLendon is his sales lady. You can always kid around with Abe. His English is not the best, but it just wouldn't be Abe Kruger if it was. He loves to kid around, and we boys claimed that when a customer wanted a blue suit of clothes, the clerk would holler back to the suit rack, "Turn on the blue lights, Abie, the man wants a blue suit." And at a shoe sale, he ran a "special" on a pair of shoes. The only trouble was, they were both right shoes. He was always good for a laugh hereabout. Abe was mayor pro tem and he loved his community. Among those citizens that should not be forgotten Abe Kruger statue should be placed around in the park with other prominent citizens that are honored there.

We have arrived at the mid-block alley. This alley is almost as much used as a street. Citizens use it as an east-west thoroughfare for "foot traffic"—mule-drawn garbage wagons. In fact, this is the preferred route for draft animals, plodding along with their creaking burdens.

You might see old Mr. Aldridge sitting in the driver's seat of his wagon, drawn by a huge brown ox, plodding toward East Pine Street, or Bert Meaker and his team of Belgian draft horses, their huge hooves clopping along the unpaved alley, their "blinders" shielding their great brown eyes from passing cars and trucks, or the Benton brothers, Northern bachelor brothers, and their teams of horses, and several others. You see, they could park behind all these stores I have mentioned and their patient animals could wait for their masters' return in relative peace.

A few repair shops and storage warehouses also open back doors to this alley that has almost become a boulevard and is also great for boys on bicycles and salvage people, referred to as rag pickers.

Now, facing Grant Street is a beautiful marble-fronted building with two magnificent marble columns, perhaps the first fine jewelry store in early Fitzgerald, John Russell's Jewelry Store, and does it shine and glitter. Jack Rouse is a local lad who has become a man and now is the proprietor. I see him with his jeweler's magnifying glass stuck in one eye, examining a customer's ailing watch.

Behind this fine marble building, a rather ramshackle wooden building, never painted and opening to the alley, is Ed Hussey's repair shop. Ed is a much-respected senior gentleman who can repair everything but a broken heart. If you have an electric fan that won't oscillate or a toaster that won't toast, take it to Ed Hussey, because he will have it humming in no time.

Ed's daughter married young Dr. D. Willcox, perhaps one of this community's most loved doctors. D. has a wonderful patient-doctor relationship. He can make you feel much better just by sitting down and talking to you.

Let's move on to Denmark Drug Co. Truly an uptown landmark. Dr. Denmark is the pharmacist. He's been here for many years, since before I was born. Arthur Denmark came to Fitzgerald in 1903. (Denmark's was located at 112 S. Grant St.)

As lots of the businesses here in the uptown, or downtown, district do, Denmark's has folding, accordion doors that can be opened in pleasant weather, so a body can just walk in off the sidewalk, which gives an informal atmosphere.

A table sits right on the front, ahead of the soda fountain, with several "drugstore" chairs. You know, the ones constructed of heavy metal wire, twisted at the corners to form designs and strong enough to support the heaviest customers. This table has become a gathering place for the town's elderly businessmen to drink a Coca-Cola or coffee at mid-morning. Most of these gentlemen are retired and getting on in years, doctors, lawyers, investors and politicians. None of them is in a hurry. The newspapers lie about and you may see a boy reading the funny papers. There are many lifetimes of wisdom resting here at this table.

Dr. Denmark is seldom not in attendance, as he has a capable staff to man his drugstore, Doris Tucker Rigdon, Joyce Howell and Mary Evelyn Barrentine can flash a smile as they make you feel right at home. They can help a man buy the correct perfume for his sweetheart or sell you a corn plaster to ease your aching feet. At the soda fountain, Bill Dorminy mixes up fresh Coca-Colas from syrup and CO_2. Ice cream treats are made with Denmark's homemade ice cream.

A young pharmacist can fill your doctor's prescriptions. This fellow's name is Dr. Ray "Red" Barfield, recently moved to Fitzgerald. His name is probably to become the name of this store. He is buying out Dr. Denmark, who is spending more and more time at the iron table. The good doctor has had a most faithful delivery man, who has pedaled his bicycle a million miles over the well-trod streets and paths to deliver medicine to the sick and lame. Why he has been with the doctor so long, everyone calls him "Jessie Denmark," but his real name is Jessie Harrell.

Jesse's only fault is his love for the finny tribe. Why,

that man would go fishing in the bath tub, and probably catch a good mess of fish, too. I am happy to see that Jessie now has a brand-new Cushman scooter to buzz around town on.

I only wish I had taken more of the advice these wise old heads have given me around this well-worn table. Jack Cooper tried his best to talk me into buying his Coca-Cola stock, which today would be worth a fortune, and I wouldn't be a tour leader. I would be afloat aboard my yacht somewhere in the Carribean. Someone would say, "Captain, aren't you from Fitzgerald?" and I would reply, "That name sounds familiar, surely I never lived there."

The lady who just parked out front and honked her horn has shocked me back to reality. I see one of the girls going out to the lady in the car, who isn't dressed to come in. Doris probably knows just what shade of lipstick she should wear and will rush it right out to her. That is what is called curb service with a million-dollar smile.

Let's move on over to the next store, Della Majors Bradshaw's dress shop. The show window has a well-dressed mannequin posing, just lifelike, in the latest style outfit right from Paris, France. Miss Della sells nothing but quality clothes. I have heard older ladies comment that they still wear clothing they bought from her 20 years ago. (Della's Shop was located at 110 S. Grant St. John Croley, Della Bradshaw's nephew, says his aunt was an original colonist, who came to the colony city from Indiana in a covered wagon. She ran her dress shop until the early to mid-1950s. The 1950 city directory shows her running the Nifty Shop at 107 S. Grant St. Her home was on S. Lee Street.)

Look both ways, my friends, and if you don't see Capt. Milton Findley and his black maria with the sirens on the front fender, let's all walk across Grant Street to the west side and stroll south. We will pick up our earlier trail here at McDonald and McDonald law firm. Angelle Stone is their young secretary. (McDonald and McDonald was located at 105 S. Grant St.)

Next door is Joe Pappas, proprietor of a cafe that, for many years, has served this community from before day till late evening. Now Joe is also a transplant, as most everyone else is whom we have seen on these streets. He is Greek, like his East Pine Street competitors. Joe has a different clientele, as his New York Cafe has a much different style. He has tables, a menu, tablecloths, waitresses, shining coffee urns, creaking ceiling fans, tile floors and a marble counter. Maybe I should say it's a sit-down cafe.

The diners quietly dabbing their mouths with linen napkins are not the blue collar workmen and floaters we saw down on E. Pine Street. These people are travelers on the Dixie Highway, professional people, social climbers, tourists and an occasional bum like me. Joe doesn't say much. I don't know if he speaks much English or he just doesn't like to chit chat. His hometown wife tends that department.

Why, you are supposed to leave a dime tip for the waitress who keeps your coffee cup full. A different atmosphere, all right, though, for my dime, Nick and Bill Pope's cafes are more fun. Oh, well, a dollar is a dollar. These boys are here to make money, not friends, although everyone loves them to pieces. (The New York Cafe was located at 109 S. Grant St. Paul says that in the forties, Fitzgerald saw a lot of tourist traffic on Grant Street, which was part of the Dixie Highway, then a main route from the north to Florida.)

Oh, look, there is Neil Peavy out in front of his marble-fronted drug store. Now, Neil is a hometown boy who grew up on the sidewalks. His father is a locomotive engineer on the Atlanta, Birmingham & Coast Railroad, but Neil didn't follow up in his dad's footsteps. He went to pharmacy school and hung out his shingle here. He is a very popular man, a natty dresser, good looking, dabbles in business around town. His store doesn't have a soda fountain, but carries a full line of cosmetics and patent medicines. He is always glad to see you and Miss Davis is his able saleslady. (Neil Drug Co. was located at 113 S. Grant.)

This town is blessed with drug stores, and we will view several more when we get around the corner and go west on Pine Street. For now, let's bid the good Neil good day before he sells us some "youth elixir" or baby powder.

Now, Neil owns some good lots out on North Grant and rumor has it that he may build a drive-in ice cream and short-order joint, called Dairy Queen, and also build his friend, Paul Ward, a new auto agency. Time will tell. Those boys are go-getters.

Put your shoes back on, ladies, you are in the city now and the master dry goods merchant, Philip Halperin, has his Surprise Store, dealing in only the best quality men's and ladies' wear. Now, don't bat an eye if the price is a little higher, but, my friend, you can be assured that when you depart these doors you have quality duds. Hart Schaffner and Marx suits, Florsheim shoes, fur coats, some goods you would find on Fifth Avenue in New York. Philip has connections there. He is not one to smoke cheap cigars either, and he must put one in his mouth when he first awakens. Philip has a great family. His children, Geraldine, Jeanette and Sammie, are most personable and loved.

His men's department is managed by Carl Findley and by Philip's brother, Jerry, and Clarence Middlebrooks. Mrs. Raymond Harris, whom I have mentioned before, is his bookkeeper, managing his accounts. Jerry Berry works here, too.

Philip Halperin should have his statue placed in the park on Central, because he has truly been an asset to this unique city.

The dress shop next door, as we move south on Grant Street, is Mrs. Kassewitz's little boutique. A small Jewish woman, she hasn't quite mastered the English language. Oh, she can talk the horns off a billy goat, but her accents are still Yiddish. She had just pushed a rack of frocks out onto the sidewalk and she will stop every woman who passes and extoll the quality and sizes. You might even negotiate special prices just because it is you. (Addie Kassewitz ran the Fashion Shop, located at 119 S. Grant.)

She knows her goods and has many friends who flock to her tiny shop. Her husband is older, Joe Kassewitz. They have several children who have excelled in high school and have gone to New York and become renamed "Doctor" and "Lawyer." Joe Kassewitz is mostly retired and is famous as a poor automobile driver. Look out when he comes down the avenue in his 1928 Dodge. If he doesn't have the right of way, he will probably take it. This is no problem, as you always see him coming because of the great clouds of smoke expelled by the old "bus" and the roar of the engine as he drives along in low gear. All the children run and the horses also are used to his daily trip through town. We love them both and hope there are always little personal shops where you feel right at home, whether you buy anything or not.

If you are a little short of funds until payday, bless these merchants' hearts, they will just smile and wrap the item up and tell you to pick up the ticket when you can. They even know your size, and also what you can afford. Reputations mean a lot on these streets.

All right, folks, from this point on, our stroll is on the home stretch. Please don't fall out on me now, as some of the best lies just before us.

If you must know the truth, I really don't believe I am capable of truly telling about our next business. It's not that I haven't spent enough time in and around this largest and busiest emporium, the 10¢ store. You just have to live with it to appreciate it as we local citizens do. Next to church on Sunday, this store has perhaps the best attendance, on Saturday, from 9 a.m. to 9 p.m. and later. Three of these stores anchor this business district—McLellan's, Delta and latecomer Dixieland compete with each other. (Delta, managed by Virgil V. Vandivere, was at 116 E. Pine in 1937 and at 121 E. Pine in 1950, while McLellan's was at 124 E. Pine. In 1937, Bart L. Pledger was manager. Robert F. Browner was the manager in 1950. The Dixieland Dime Store actually came a little later.)

Now, I am no sage or fortune teller or a lion of the business world, but my observation has been that a town will never amount to much and become much unless it has a dime store. Not that people buy so much, though they do.

If a farm family were in a pickup truck on Saturday afternoon, headed for town, and there was a good general store just two miles up the road, which was paved, and the pavement ended at that settlement, and a muddy, rough track led to a bustling town that had a dime store, and they had a gallon or two of gas, they would rattle away to the dime store, to buy a new piece of oil cloth for the kitchen table or maybe a piece of linoleum for the floor, an Aladdin mantel for the lamp, some icicles or a string of lights for the Christmas tree, a "Blue Horse" tablet for school, a pair of sandals that would come to pieces at the first rain, a goldfish and bowl, a turtle with a palm tree painted on its shell, or a white paper bag filled with coconut bonbons at the candy counter. (Paul notes that dime stores were the Wal-Marts of their day. Aladdin mantels were mantels for kerosene lanterns that made the lantern give out about twice the light of an ordinary lantern, Paul says.)

There was a lunch counter, where you could sit on a stool and watch a lady in a uniform cook you a hamburger or corn dog. Man, now that's living, country come to town on a Saturday afternoon. Wonder what they are doing at that dusty ol' store at the crossroads named Rebecca, all festooned with cobwebs, where an ol' bald-headed clerk waits with a barrel of stale old "penny wheel" crackers.

Hey there, fellow with that truckload of hogs, how about catching a ride to Fitzgerald with you? So we can go to the dime store and the picture show and maybe on down to the Greek Cafe. We will get back here the best way we can. Surely someone will be coming this way. And we won't be late for church in the morning.

How can you keep them down on the farm after they have seen gay old Fitzgerald and the dime store?

OK, come on back to the corner of Grant and Pine Street. McLellan's is managed by Allen Wages. Ruby Haskins is head bookkeeper and Mrs. Revels works with her. And is that Robert Matthews, a floor walker? Data Young and Betty Jean Hinson are at the candy counter. If one of them likes you, she will drop two or three extra pieces in your bag. I don't know the ladies at the snack bar. School girls are sales ladies. They don't make much, but they get to see everybody. Romance can bloom at a 5¢ and 10¢ store. Many a heart has beat a little faster when that special fellow walked in, whether he purchased anything or not. Girls stroll in to buy hair pins and fingernail polish, dye to change the color of a blouse—Rit, I believe.

Some old guy might need some electric wire or a plug-in. If it isn't at the 10¢ store, it probably isn't made in Japan or China. Nothing was supposed to cost more than a dime, but that was before the war. Things are cheaper in these stores, but the quality may leave something to be desired. The girls' wages fall in that category also, after 12 long, footsore hours, they open their pay envelopes and get $2 or less.

Dime store, 5 and 10, variety shop, whatever you choose to call it, the store is not only a hub for bargain hunters, but a social center for all ages. Tiny tots and kids, eyes wide, stand at the toy counter. Boys buy model airplane kits, ready to assemble. Why, you might even need a checker board, store bought, maybe even Chinese checkers, Monopoly, light bulbs, half soles for your shoes and the glue to attach them or heel taps, so that when you walk down the sidewalk they will go "click click." Many hands are shaken, many necks are hugged right among the merchandise.

Don't forget your flashlight batteries. It will be late when that pretty young saleslady who promised to let you walk her home gets off work, clutching that brown pay envelope.

Now, if I may have your attention. Outside the store on the Grant Street side, you will see that the brick wall that forms the east side of McLellan's has a side entrance and a small show window, with a display fitting to the season. At Easter there will be paper mache Easter bunnies and some made of chocolates on display on a bed of green artificial moss. After Easter, you can buy them very cheap and put them on a high shelf in your closet, and the kids will love them next Easter, just like they were new. There is a small water cooler just inside the side door, a great oasis on a hot afternoon. "Meet you at the water cooler at 10 o'clock"—no telling how many times that statement has been heard. Now, don't be late or I may leave with ol' sport over there.

Now, if I may have your more serious attention. We have just won a terrible war, all over the world, and we barely won it, thanks to hundreds of boys who left these sidewalks, possibly a thousand. They gave their youth, freedom and many, their lives, to preserve this lifestyle that I have tried to describe. Starting at the time of Pearl Harbor, a local man by the name of Wade Malcolm has tirelessly painted on this wall the name of each man who left this town to go to places that we had never heard of.

Some were gone for four years. Many were wounded. Quite a few laid down their young lives. Now, in 1946, the entire brick wall, perhaps 100 feet, is covered by names, row on row. By the wounded soldiers' names is a silver star, which also marks those missing in action. And bless their precious hearts, Wade painted a gold star by the names of those who died. Time and weather will fade this heroes' display and it will soon be illegible, but hopefully the names will never be forgotten.

As we leave the dime store, moving west, on the right-hand sidewalk is the Darling Shop, a dress shop. My knowledge of dress shops is very limited, but it is a nice shop.

Across the street on the south side is McConnell's cloth store, another "chain" business. This store specializes in cloth, yard goods and patterns, sewing supplies, etc., as many women still make or sew their own and their children's clothes. Mrs. Handley is the manager, and I see Ruby Morehead, sales lady. (McConnell's actually came along a few years after this.)

While we are looking over to this side of the street, let's not overlook Butch Whittle's pool room, a long-standing entertainment establishment. Now, Butch lost his leg in a railroad derailment recently and he, being the well liked fellow he is, has many friends who pass a few hours honing their skills at the green felt tables. Lots of citizens, men who keep books, work as salesmen or farm compete with one another for mostly fun and camaraderie. A few sharks exist, but by far, the majority just relaxes. Woodrow Reeves moves from table to table with the rack to start new games and collect the money that pays for the game. He is known as a "rack man." Butch has an easy smile for everyone on the sidewalk. Hope to see him around for many years to come.

Over on our side of Pine Street, we are standing in front of the National Drug Store, owned and operated by

Dr. Register and his young son, Jack. The street front, again, consists of folding glass doors that can be opened, in good weather, right on the sidewalk, much as with Denmark Drugs on Grant Street. There is a table right on the sidewalk, just out of the traffic pattern. The crowd that sits around this table is about the same crowd that frequents Denmark's. They must migrate back and forth. Most of them have been here since colony days, or about then, and very little, good or bad, has failed to come under their scrutiny. We young fellows refer to them as the forefathers or "silver foxes" because of their gray hair (if any) and their wisdom. Again, here are the fine lines of candy, cosmetics and over-the-counter and prescription drugs.

The soda fountain is among the best and the "jerks" who wait on the customers have a towel tied around their waists, which is the mark of a soda jerk.

Since 1929, times—financial times, that is—had been, to say the least, hard. Even "landed" gentry had no cash money. Barter was common. Clothes were patched. Notes were overdue. Tax was unpaid. Farmers had plenty to eat, but hard money was almost non-existent. The railroad company missed two periods. No cash, boys, just have to live out of the "grab," an old coach converted into a commissary with only necessities. (Paul says they took the seats out of the coach and made a store out of it, selling flour, lard, hoop cheese, baking soda, castor oil, work shoes, etc. It was well stocked with staple goods and trains pulled it from community to community, Cordele, Montezuma, Byron, all along the line. "It amounted to getting it on credit," he says. "It kept the employees supplied even though the railroad couldn't pay them.")

The Great Depression didn't overlook Fitzgerald. When President Roosevelt came to Fitzgerald, he told everyone that things were going to get better. There would be a chicken in every pot and the railroad would pay its workers every penny it owed them. Just hold on, boys, good times are right around the corner.

Things slowly got better. My dad bargained to buy a new 1939 Chevrolet, and we had a telephone put in. Now, weren't we in high cotton?

And here and now, I must tell you of a custom that existed in Fitzgerald equally at the three drug stores that have full-service soda fountains—Denmark's, National and the Central Pharmacy around on Central and Main. Now, gather around all you footsore sightseers, I am about to tell you not of the midnight ride of Paul Revere, but the mid-morning ride of the high society ladies of our town.

Along about then, when things were getting better, before the war, the ladies of the town would call four or five other ladies and invite them to be picked up at about 10 a.m. The groups of housewives, having gotten the kids off to school and dinner warming on the electric stove, would put on a fresh cotton frock, powder their noses, dab a little lipstick on their lips, drive uptown, park in front of one of the uptown drugstores, honk the horn and out would come the soda jerk or his helper.

With the windows rolled down, the ladies would order fountain Coca-Colas and pretzels, maybe a cherry Coke or vanilla Coke. The lady who did the calling would put the change to settle the bill on the tray that the jerk hung on the window. She was the hostess. If the young man brought paper napkins and straws, she might even tip him a dime. They would have a great old time, laugh and talk, crank up in about 30 minutes, rush home and have lunch on the table at 12 o'clock because hubby and the kids would be dashing in to eat. (Paul says that the ladies who enjoyed the "mid-morning ride" were established married women in their 30s and 40s. "It ended with the war," he says. "There was no gas, no tires. The Depression was over, but the war brought these shortages.")

Yes, old Franklin Roosevelt and his New Deal had

begun to work. Paychecks were good, the banks were open, loaning money, and cash registers were beginning to jingle. Happy times were here again. People could pay bills with hard money instead of with hen eggs, hams and cane syrup.

Was that young Jesse Whitten driving LD. Wright's store truck by, headed for the country, loaded down with flour, sugar, salt, vanilla flavoring, candy for the children—Mary Janes, Tootsie Rolls, Baby Ruths—and empty chicken crates stacked as high as they could go. The truck has hinged steps that he can let down in the back and farmers come in and shop. Jesse will return to Mr. Wright's store on West Suwannee Street tonight, loaded down with eggs, butter, side meat, hams and those chicken coops stuffed with squawking chickens, which will end up in town folks' pots, just as FDR promised. (Through this bartering, shopkeepers were able to offer their city customers fresh farm produce, Paul says.)

Why, one dime store manager told me he took in as much money from 6 p.m. to 9 p.m. on Saturday evening as he did the whole week.

People were on these sidewalks, here on Pine Street, like sardines in a can, thicker than hairs on a dog's back and most everyone had a few green backs in their new overalls or pocket books. Fewer wagons are in the vacant lots; Bennie Anderson has sold them Ford V-8's, J. Gould Williams is putting them in Chevrolets and the "whole cheese," Harry Vinson hawking his Dodges, Plymouths and Chryslers. The mule traders have fallen on hard times. They better start, and have, selling used cars and trucks.

Back to our stroll—as I look across the street, I see I have failed to mention a "private bank" opened by Mr. Preston Murray, next to the vacant old bank on the corner. The money changers are having their day. New banks are springing up.

From where we stand, I see Horace White, one of the

most popular barbers, has opened his own barber shop, a nice roomy shop. He has four chairs and a brisk trade. You nearly always have to wait your turn, for Horace to "pop" that sheet he has knotted around a customer's shoulders. When he calls "next" you had better jump up and take your seat. Looks like Red Raines and Walter Owens are working here. Big Boy Hall may be opening a shop of his own down the street.

Things change so fast. Every time you come uptown, new shops are opening. Forgive me if I'm not up to date.

Next door is Hargroves Shoe Shop, a popular place whether your shoes need repair or not. Dick Hargroves is a cobbler, but his claim to fame is four sons, Gordon, Reggie, Billy and Lauren. They are fine young men and all have been fine athletes. Football is the sport of choice in Fitzgerald, and all four have done well, but the youngest, Lauren, is All-American material. He will put Fitzgerald on the map.

Dock Boggus, who has returned from the war, and his wife, Martha, have moved into part of the building the shoe shop is in, and they have opened a jewelry store here. This is the first year for Dock's Credit Jewelry, but I think they will be here for awhile.

As we thread our way west, here on the south side of Pine Street, the last business before the mid-block alley is the last dime store of those I mentioned earlier. Somewhat smaller than the other two, the Delta 5 and 10 is a good place to find a bargain. Mr. Vandivere and his sister, Miss Esther, manage it. It isn't quite as up to date and has fewer clerks and a quieter atmosphere.

I really don't know if I have enough paper to jot down the history and character of this next store. I hope I can select the correct adjectives to express the service and flavor that this drug store, and its popular lunch room, add to the pleasures of life. A friendly, at-home atmosphere has abounded here since the settlement of the first colonists arriving from the north. What would downtown Fitzgerald be without Dr. Will Haile's Haile Drug Co.?

He is on his last legs, but his able staff is ever adding on to its reputation as a home away from home. Why, I wouldn't feel like I had been uptown if I hadn't visited my friends and elders here. It is always open, it seems. If it isn't, you can hang out in front. "Meet you at Haile's" is the password. Adventures start here. If they sold tickets to Pine Street, this is where you would buy them.

Could I say, don't miss this elephant sitting in the front hall that leads to downtown? I get excited just telling you about it. The large cast-iron stove with the stove pipe wired to the ceiling, with buckets or scuttles filled with coal waiting to be chunked into the hot embers and several characters from the past warming their hands or back sides. Look out—you are smoking!

A roaring exhaust fan blows in summer. Here you can get advice for every problem that may rear its ugly head, advice on your health, from poison ivy to an ingrown toenail or even a hangover. Dr. J.W. Fountain, Dr. Thurston Ashley and Dr. Horace Chambless are always busy filling prescriptions but are very kind to ailing people of all walks of life, all colors, all ages. Yes, if you just need a friend's smile or handshake, head for Haile's Drug Store.

The large lunch room is as large as a cafe, occupying half the store, separated by a partition. Richard Gibbs and Mary Gibbs manage the lunch room with its line of booths on one side wall and a fountain counter on the other wall, with a large table seating probably a dozen citizens, from the mayor to retired railroad men, to lawyers and used car salesmen and even preachers. Why, Brother Winn is head bookkeeper at Haile's. (Paul says that Haile's served fast food—hamburgers, sandwiches and such—as well as breakfast.)

You can get a banana split or a salad and the special

of the day, perhaps for a dollar. Enough coffee is drunk at that back table to float a battleship and you can get all the latest news there, long before it is documented by the local newspapers. The Macon and Atlanta papers are always scattered about, some loafer working the crossword puzzle.

You will hear nicknames such as Bozo, High Pockets, Windy, Bear, Dude, Speedy, Kid, Hollywood, Sharp, Rags, Moon, Slug, Hump, Shotgun, Rat, Pug, Smokie, Professor, Doc, Counselor, Boon, Jigs, Captain, Colonel, Snog, Bum, Ironhead, Spike, Ears, Kid Gloves, Frog, Romeo, Cornbread, Babe, Jet Job, Mule Mouth, Buckshot, Slick, Skin, Snerd and Half-a-Bucket.

One brilliant lawyer, perhaps the most brilliant legal mind in town is here, too. Everyone said he had been admitted to the bar in 1910 and never left. His wife has an umbrella with a sharp point on the end. She will prod him home, and you had better give him plenty of room on the sidewalk, because he is going from one side to the other. What a waste. He is good for a quick legal opinion if you can't afford a lawyer. Just another one of the characters who abound here. Why, even I might have gotten more education at that back table than I did in all high school, even a degree in romance, which was never far away.

The store side, in the front, is a post office substation, which is very convenient. You can buy stamps, mail letters and packages.

Starling Owens, a retired railroad conductor and Mr. and Mrs. Mike Chalker sit in the little cage-like office. (Janet Willingham, Sarah Joyce Walker, Betty Young and Lucille Walker all worked in this branch office at different times.)

Last, but not least, Janet Willingham, Maxine Handley, Barbara Anne Snowden, Margaret Warbington and others combine beauty and service as sales ladies. Billy McGowan is the friendly delivery boy.

Out front, on the sidewalk entrance is a pair of

scales, the kind you stand on, drop a penny in the slot and get your weight and fortune. The "fortune" part is now broken, but the scales make a fine place for a young fellow to stand and review the pedestrians as they pass. These fellows probably won't buy anything, but they group up here to get acquainted with young ladies who have ventured into town. One of you boys, be sure and stand on those scales, one of you young blades, so they don't float away. Robert Matthews and Paul Dunn have done their share of standing on them, and they aren't checking their weight.

Well, I'll be a horn-toed biddy if Bowen Shepherd, a relative of Mr. W.R. Bowen, isn't coming down the sidewalk, pushing his Snow Ball cart. Mounted on bicycle wheels with a striped canvas top and a rack of bottles containing colored liquid and fruit syrup, Bowen has a 50¢ block of ice in the middle of his cart, a metal scraper to shave ice and conical paper cups to hold the shaved ice. He is headed east on Pine Street to set up and sell snow cones, 20¢ each, select your flavor. He is a great fellow and operated Bowens Mill's recreation center. He is always laughing, a friend to everyone, young and old alike. Bowen is a hard worker and always has a new project. He told me that he made more money with that old snow cone cart than any other venture of his. Bowen's spirit will never perish.

From this sidewalk, standing in front of Haile's, is probably the premiere spot to people watch. Sooner or later, the characters will parade by and there isn't even a circus in town. But who needs a circus when you have Pine Street in Fitzgerald on a Saturday afternoon?

Here comes H. Pennington Gibbs stepping off like a drum major, sample case in hand. Don't stop him, or he will sell you a pair of Knapp shoes. He makes a living selling these fine shoes. He has customers all over South Georgia and probably has walked around the world several times. He goes to other towns on the Greyhound bus, always in his neat suit, coat and tie. Good man, good shoes. What a combination. (Paul recalls that Gibbs lived on W. Pine Street and worked a route of regular customers, though he was always open to new customers.)

If we wait long enough, the old scissors sharpener will pass, small suitcase in hand, a small older man, just a little shabby. I never heard his name. He lives out of town, knocks on doors to sharpen housewives' knives and shears. He calls on barber shops also. He has a grinder mounted in that black suitcase, and he can set up shop in the twinkle of an eye. He never says a word, just turns the handle to his grinder. I doubt if he will ever retire, as he must be 100 years old. What a career!

Upstairs over a store on Main Street, a block from here, lives a great character. He dresses in the same clothes that were in style in 1895, the year Fitzgerald was founded: celluloid collar, bow tie, button-up, high-topped shoes with spats, his little black hat a derby, of course, set at a jaunty angle on his gray head. He has a walking cane with a brass handle. He is affectionately known to everyone as "Uncle Gabe" Waters, Homer Waters' father. He tiptoes along the sidewalk, tipping his hat to ladies. As he passes us boys, he always says, "Could one of you boys spare a dear old man a dime for a cup of coffee?" But a cup of coffee doesn't cost but a nickel. Uptown would never be the same without Uncle Gabe. He needs to be on the stage. Here, take this dime, dear fellow, and tell me a tale of the long, long ago. A dime well spent.

If our timing is right, we might see Allen Spires, the local axe handle producer, coming in from a few days' camping in the Ocmulgee River swamp. He arrives in his Old International flatbed truck with no cab, just a box for the driver to sit on, the windshield sticking up, the flatbed loaded with hickory and white oak bolts (logs) cut to axe handle lengths, camping gear, dogs and his husky son, the one called "Lunk" sitting beside him. They come up Pine Street to drop off old "river rat" Tilman Murphy, a good friend who caught a ride in to spend the weekend with his daughter, who lives across from the jail. He and Allen are the last of the stout-hearted men who floated rafts of virgin pine logs down the river to Darien to the saw mills and walked back the 120 miles back to Camp Brooklyn, near town. Tilman never drove a motor vehicle, as far as I know. He now lives on the river and sells catfish to people who come to his camp.

Allen has a large house and yard on the railroad track and splits out handles, jacks up his truck and puts a belt to the rear wheel and he and the "boys" hold the blanks up to his homemade sander and can expertly shape an axe or hammer handle to perfection. Boat paddles, also. He has a large shaving pile that we kids loved to play on. He never ran us off or fussed at us.

He has cages with wild animals—coons, even wildcats. It's just an adventure to visit his premises. Who can forget a gruff, kind-hearted old man who just loves to work?

As we look about for the people who call these streets home and who give some personality to cold, hard bricks and concrete, we should look upstairs over these thriving businesses, as stairways open onto the sidewalk, like the one that leads up to Mrs. Lucy Owens' photographic studio. She has recorded on film many citizens and their families, since settlement days. (In 1950, Mrs. Owens' studio was at 120 1/2 E. Pine St. In 1937, her studio was at 205 S. Main St.)

Dr. J.E. McMillan, perhaps one of the area's best-loved physicians, has his medical office above Haile's Drug Co. (His office was at 110 1/2 E. Pine St.) He is semi-retired now, but in days past he delivered many babies and set many a broken arm. He loves to farm and still has his farm at Osierfield, and I have, many times, gone just outside town, where he has a pig pen, to feed his hogs. He is on the street every day around Haile's. He is a friend to all, and if your name has slipped his mind, he will just call you "baby." A man of the people.

I wish "Sister" Ella Mae McCarty would stop blowing the horn in that big blue Buick that Monroe Fletcher sold her husband, Jim McCarty, the quiet Gulf Oil distributor. She is a much-loved dowager lady, a lot of fun and lovable, but her driving here uptown leaves a little to be desired to say the least. She is double-parked down in front of Dick Hargroves' shoe shop, blowing her horn for him to bring her the shoes he has repaired for her. She will park anywhere she decides to. Blow again, Sister Ella Mae, ol' Dick is probably running that grinder and can't hear you.

Here comes Mr. Findley, the traffic police. That's what he is paid for, you know. Stay at that soda fountain, Roy Boles, it isn't the ladies blowing for curb service.

Johnny Seanor has a Plymouth coupe, maybe a 1936 model, restored and tuned to perfection, but he will wait till Saturday afternoon to creep through town here on Pine Street, idled down to walking speed. Hey, Johnny, look at all the cars behind you. Speed up! I hope Homer Waters and his buddies don't show up with the bucking Ford.

I need to tend to my business as tour leader now and tell you to look across the street. You are looking at the Western Auto store, owned and managed by A.A. Boggus, "Double A" as he is known. The Sowell brothers, Bill and Jim, are the clerks in this store.

This store has automotive accessories, home appliances and, don't forget, Western Flyer bicycles, fishing tackle, tires of all kinds. You might call it an emporium. A busy place, occupying several once-vacant storefronts. These automobiles are the rage since the war ended. Go on in and get you a radio, rear-view mirror or maybe mud flaps, doll the old bus up a little. Good times are here, let 'em roll.

Double A has a son, Argin, and daughter, Evelyn, who are friends and school mates of mine, great kids, just hometown folks.

There was a saying in the past, "If you can't pull with your neighbors, pull out." I hope that spirit never changes.

Durden's Electric Store is next. Charlie Durden and his wife, Cleolas, work hard to satisfy their many customers, selling music, radios, records, record players, electric supplies and machines.

Charlie is also a surveyor and has laid off lots and subdivisions. Their children, Jane and Charles, have been raised in this store and teenagers are always welcome to come in and hear the latest hit records by Patti Page, the Mills Brothers, Patsy Cline, Kitty Wells and Eddy Arnold.

We will need to mount the stairs to go up to the offices above the businesses I have just described. Several are vacant now. But the ones that remain are much alive and thriving. The dark hall, after you climb the creaking old stairs, has half-glass doors that have names written on them, names from the past. The knobs have been turned by many hands that now lie folded in rest out at Evergreen or other cemeteries, hands that came to pay rent, house payments and insurance. Calloused hands that counted out hard-earned money or were folded humbly asking for credit or a small loan.

This is the office of the J.B. Seanor Co., offering insurance and property for rent. The original Seanors are gone. Their son, Preston Seanor, is an officer in the Army and his wife, Orleans Humphreys Seanor, is now behind the desk, every inch a lady. She is assisted by a young lady by the name of Jeanette McDaniel, a recent graduate of Irwin County High School down at Mystic. The pecan groves and blueberry plantings are managed by Mrs. Seanor's son, Johnny, the one with the Plymouth coupe, and Jackie Farmer, a strong, capable high school senior, as most of the young men have been gone to war. Several of us school boys have helped her, including Cecil Rigdon and yours truly. Orleans has been like a mother to several of us young "sprouts." She also has a young daughter, Lauren, who is being groomed to ladyhood by her mother and grandmother, Mrs. Humphreys. (Paul says the blueberries were originally grown by the senior Seanors for a winery in Cordele—a venture that was ended by Prohibition.)

Col. William Grigsby, an attorney, has his law office up here, too.

If we were to step down the hall, a bit farther, and open the door that says "Jim Jones, Justice of the Peace," we would see the judge sitting in his swivel chair, thumbing through the latest batch of garnishments, convictions, peace warrants, etc., handing the papers to his trusty bailiff, Mr. "Big" Maddox. I never heard Mr. Maddox's given name, but he sure got the right nickname. That man is big. His suit of clothes looks like a circus tent and his broad-brimmed black hat speaks of authority to the worst of them, and there are a few. He has a rather old model car and fills up the front seat. I hope he doesn't have any paper for me. He uses his claw hammer to tack a notice to a door. (The bailiff served eviction notices and summons to court for the justice of the peace.)

He lives at the end of North Main Street, by the Legion home that sits in the corner of the park known as Legion Park. A large covey of quail abide among the giant virgin pines that soar aloft there. We boys once posted a lookout to watch for Mr. Maddox's old car. We would shoot the quail and run before he could get cranked and apprehend us. Our mothers would sure be proud of the two or three quail we brought in for supper. We never told the whole story, or got caught. Fitzgerald was a bird sanctuary and it was against the law to shoot birds here, but you had to be fast to catch us.

By the way, Jim Jones loves to quail hunt and he would loan us his bird dog, Rex. Old Rex would always swallow the first quail you shot, but never laid a tooth into another bird, all day. Just his fee, I reckon. Jim is probably too busy to talk to us, even if we went upstairs.

Downstairs, below these offices, is Rhomelle Patterson's popular beauty salon, Rhomelle's. A local girl, she and her sister Gladys have been at this location, next to Bradshaws, for a long time. This is a very busy shop and she is a very popular lady.

We have been anchored here in front of Haile's Drug Co. and must move on if we are to finish our stroll today. Mrs. Newton has a hat shop here and does a good business—you ladies must have new hats to go with your Easter outfits. I see Callie Sue Ward inside now, making a selection. (Margaret Newton's women's clothing store was located at 110 E. Pine St., where Hybernia's was to be at a later date.)

I fall short on describing these dress shops and beauty shops as men seldom darken their hallowed doors, but I know there are fine clerks like Iva Glenn Mitchell, Gerry Tucker and Maxine Wilson, who can assist any bewildered man who wanders into a dress shop in search of a gift for his wife.

The Great Atlantic and Pacific Tea Company store is a very modern and popular store. It is managed by E.G. Scott and Gladys Greer and Johnnie (Mrs. Haynes) Moorehead are cashiers. Jimmy Mahoney works here in the produce department. This store is one of the "See No Failure Stops" for local housewives on their weekly grocery shopping trips. (Paul says "see no failure" is railroad talk for instructions that are important and must be obeyed.) It's the A&P for short and specializes in fresh-ground coffee. They have the blend to suit the most selective coffee drinker and will grind the beans before your eyes and pour the ground coffee into red bags with the words "8 O'clock Coffee" printed on them. Now, how can you beat that for freshness, without going to Brazil? They have a full line of fancy canned goods, fresh fruit and great bananas. Mr. Scott's friendly smile has won many a customer. Pull your buggy on over to Mrs. Greer's checkout stall and be sure and come back next week.

The A&P occupies part of a large three-story building covering this corner of Pine and Main street. It is quite a large building, the second or third largest here. Most of the building is occupied by the Piedmont Hotel, operated by a most genteel couple of middle-aged people, Mr. and Mrs. R.I. Maffet. As with most corner buildings along here, the main entrance opens to Pine Street and a lesser entrance opens to South Main. The lobby is at the Pine Street entrance, furnished with over-stuffed sofas and chairs, with magazine racks and reading lamps ornamented with fringed shades. An L-shaped check-in counter is beside the wide stairs that lead to the guest rooms on the second and third floors above. There is no elevator. Mr. Maffet is the desk clerk, with a cheery smile for everyone. Double, glass French doors open into a spacious well-lighted dining room with the ever-present ceiling fans thrashing the air.

Here comes Mrs. Maffet, a generously built lady, emerging from the kitchen that occupies the entire rear of the building. Her glowing personality would brighten the darkest room. She can smile and make you feel right at home, as she leads you to a table covered with a white linen tablecloth, set with napkins folded to resemble a crown and silverware placed beside each place. She might even, and usually does, sit down and chat with you for a spell. Her waitresses, in uniforms and white shoes, bring tall, frosty glasses of iced tea. After you have made your selection from the menu, a salad is set before you and in no time your dinner is brought to your table by the attractive waitress, the entree on a generous china plate, the side orders in small bowls, with a platter of biscuits or cornbread, all set on the table. The dining room is well patronized. People are in no hurry and enjoy each other's company until, at last, dessert and a cup of coffee are served.

On Sundays, after church, the lobby is full of would-be diners waiting for a table. We didn't eat here often as it is not cheap, about $1.25, and surely you would leave a dime tip on the table.

(Paul says that most of the customers at Fitzgerald's hotels were traveling salesmen who came on the trains, though each hotel boasted a few permanent residents. The salesmen would take orders all over town for several days, for clothes, shoes, jewelry, whatever they might be selling. They would also go out into the county to the country stores. At the Piedmont, only a few of the guest rooms had private baths. The rest of the guests used common bathrooms located at the end of each hall. The Lee-Grant, which had high ceilings, elegant furnishings and ceiling fans in every bedroom, and the Piedmont were Fitzgerald's nicest hotels, though the Jeff Davis had been a nice hotel in its day. Paul recalls that the Lee-Grant even had bellhops. "They might even have had a telephone that you could use," he says with a grin.)

As we depart the Piedmont dining room and look across Pine Street, we see the Bradshaw Music Company, one of Fitzgerald's earliest businesses.

Could I remind you that Fitzgerald is a young town, as towns go, established in 1895, here among the virgin pines in what had been Creek Indian territory until 1820—not much more than 100 years ago. The town is only 50 years old. All this development and business in a mere blink of Father Time's eye.

Oscar Bradshaw and his brother, Charlie, and their sister, Miss Ozella, are leading citizens and business people. Mr. Bradshaw's store manager was Mr. John Croley. Young Zebedee Parsons and Perry Rodgers are salesmen who know the line of goods. The company was built on the popular piano sales. Every church and school, and many homes, is proud of their piano.

Since the war, the sale of electric stoves, washing machines, freezers, refrigerators and other household appliances has only strengthened this business. It's always a pleasure to visit Bradshaw Music. Mr. O.L. is a fixture here beside the Jay, Garden and Jay law firm that occupies the southeast corner of Pine and Main.

This law office is housed in a stone and masonry building that has dominated this corner all my life. Tall palm trees rise high above the sidewalk on the Main Street side, down to where Bradshaw's side entrance opens to Main Street. Col. Jay is renowned for his real estate titles, having searched and recorded them since Colony days. His partner, Col. Allen Garden, is the courtroom lawyer and young Harvey Jay is solicitor of the court, or district attorney. Young Clayton Jay has returned from his tour of duty in the Army and has joined the law firm as a junior partner. Good to have you back, "Bubba." Fitzgerald needs to retain her enterprising, educated young men to guide her progress in the future.

We have about finished our sojourn on East Pine Street, South Grant Street, South Sherman Street and South Sheridan, which comprises the walking business district of our little city.

As we stand here on the corner of South Main and Pine, let's take a few steps south. I believe we can see a few points of interest without much walking below the hallowed walls of Jay, Garden and Jay.

A brand-new bus station has arisen. Leon Harrell is the agent for Greyhound and Trailways bus operators. Dr. Ward has opened a medical office in the Alligood home place. (The Alligood home place was at 216 S. Main.)

If you look a block to the south, Miss Inez McLauchlin has sold her antebellum-styled, columned home to Jimmie Paulk for the new Paulk Funeral Home.

It is just across the corner from the First Baptist Church. The church is an impressive structure built of cream-colored brick with a sheet metal dome. Constructed in the early days of the city, she bears her age well. From here, lovely houses line South Main Street, but that is another tour, for another day.

Cast your eyes on the wooden structure back this way. It is the WRC (Women's Relief Corps) Hall, built as a meeting place for this organization of patriotic women. It was among the first permanent structures raised by the first settlers. The metallic tapping sound coming from there, that I have been trying to talk above, is the sound of the students in Anne Stokes' dancing school. The stolid ladies of the WRC would turn over in their graves if they saw the "budding dancers," Johnnie Miller, Connie Leverett, Nancy Hart, the Brown twins and many, many more, practicing for their review at the Grand Theatre, up on the stage. Rattle those ancient timbers as Mrs. Jake Miller and Polly Winn for many years tickled the piano ivories, flit like butterflies, you ballet students. Go on to Broadway. You may even end up a Rockette at Radio City Music Hall, who knows?

Up closer is the budding auto business of T.H. Stone, the Chrysler dealer, with a showroom up front and a shop managed by Joe Simmons.

T.H.'s wife, Ruth, is usually around, and is that young Jerry Wilson, a "foreigner" from Irwin County, behind the parts counter?

Hudson White is selling those new TV sets like ol' Chuck is selling hot cakes at the Snack Shop around the corner. Radios will just have to take a rest.

Wait for a green light and cross over to the west side of South Main Street. Here is another two-story building, built by Dr. Holtzendorf, now deceased. This half block, up to the alley, was burnt to the ground in 1935. The modern Grand Theatre and its satellite shops and stores burnt down and lay smoldering for a week. I was but a lad when late one night my parents woke me, bundled me up and we walked up the ever-walked, no-name, east-west alley that bisects uptown to the Carnegie Library building, and I stood in a vacant lot across from the White Swan laundry and watched the leaping flames consume the half-block area. Flaming boards swept skyward and sparks showered the surrounding area. No fireworks show ever equaled that fire, unless you count the burning of Parker-Higdon's wholesale grocery, down on the railroad tracks above here (at 120 N. Main, where the post office is now), which burned a few years later. Canned goods exploded for weeks after that fire was over.

We must have had a great fire department to save the adjoining buildings. Willie Crawford, Willie Brewer, Dean Mitcham, Mr. Rawlins, Elmer Livingston, Webster Dix, Wade Cleary, the Norris brothers and Gene and Ed Davis, laid-off railroad men, Bob Dykes, and others, saved the town on many occasions.

Martin Theatres owned the "picture show" building and soon rebuilt the entire property. I couldn't believe it, but it truly rose from its own ashes, to everyone's delight.

I am getting ahead of myself, though. We still have an important structure here on the corner of Pine and Main Street—two stories, with a stairway on the right side leading up to Dr. Cornwell's office. A mass of ailing humanity has mounted these stairs, to be diagnosed and treated by the good doctor. He just appeared here on the scene, during the trying days of wartime. The old doctors, Dorminy and the Ware brothers, Coffee (the eye, ear, nose and throat specialist), McMillan and Fussell had either died or were retired or semi-retired. Dr. Cornwall, in his white shirt, suit pants, black suspenders and horn-rimmed glasses, was in his prime and a God-send to Fitzgerald.

Ina Coffee is his receptionist. He will leave the office with his coat slung over his shoulder, black bag in hand. He doesn't have time to gab, he is just always on call.

Two businesses have occupied the ground floor for several years. Ralph Adams has opened the Main Street Pharmacy since his return from the War. A popular ice cream parlor and sandwich shop is located here also, run by the Luke sisters, catering to movie goers and other pleasure seekers, who find the Mecca to be a friendly and convenient gathering spot. Julia Tucker worked at the grill when she was but a girl. Lots of laughs and smiles here. Everyone likes to stick his head in at the Mecca, maybe just to shoot the pinball machine. Look out, don't bump me or it will go to tilt, and I was just before getting a free game. Great snacks and camaraderie here. (The Mecca preceded the Main Street Pharmacy in the same building.)

Several storefronts present themselves before the ticket booth and lobby entrance to the picture show, as it is commonly known. Properly it is the Grand Theatre, as the high, flashing neon sign beacons, day and evening.

First, let's not overlook the stalls or shops flanking the Grand—an insurance office, Lee's and Chalker's sandwich shops, and Hunter's jewelry store. (In 1950, Arthur Lee's sandwich shop was located at 125 S. Main, sharing space with Elmo Downing's Globe Store, which sold books. J.C. Hunter had the Fitzgerald Jewelry Store at 123 S. Main.)

The optometry office of Dr. John McCord, a solid citizen, is along here. He has perhaps fitted more eyeglasses than there are peas in the pods of five-acres of peas. "Doc" and his tiny wife, Lois, are the kind of people who make this town a great place to live.

Let's take time out for a few street characters, like Mr. Terry and Blind Brooks' peanut roaster, with the little whistle tweeting when the nuts are hot. He is an old man, but don't know anything about retiring, smiling at passers by as he bags fresh-roasted peanuts in five- and 10-cent bags. He does a brisk business as is evident from the peanut shells scattered about the street and sidewalk. They smell about as good as the popcorn that is dancing about in the popper inside the theatre lobby, but you must buy a ticket to go into the show, while there is a never-ending show going on here on the sidewalk, in front.

There is a bicycle rack which serves to park your bike while you are inside, or as a metal perch to roost on and see who has show fare. There are no free passes and Mr. I.T. Taylor is a dignified manager. Mr. Gilbert Goldwire is the local manager, who will patrol this area if the crowd gets too loud.

Miss Ida Taylor, who has a lifetime contract to sell tickets, probably wouldn't win the Miss Congeniality contest at the Miss America pageant. Everyone loves her, but I wish I could say the same for her love of the public, especially teenage boys who love to aggravate her. Shame on you, boys. She's here to sell tickets, not to make friends. Ann Mathis and Miss Fletcher sell tickets and L.C. Fussell and Charlie Law run the projector. Jack Farmer, a schoolboy grown tall, is tearing tickets at the end of the lobby. You keep your half of your ticket to prove your purchase or to be excused and re-admitted. Gerald Hardin also takes up tickets here. Francis Raynor is an assistant manager.

I could spend a week trying to tell you of the cowboy and Indian wars, how many stagecoach wheels went off cliffs, the many roads to wherever that Bob Hope and Bing Crosby have taken Dorothy Lamour down, how many musicals have been sung and how many Alfred Hitchcock mysteries have been shown. There are vampires, wolf men, Frankenstein, Dracula and, always, Tarzan, Jane and Boy, out-swimming crocodiles. Leo, the Metro-Goldwyn-Mayer (MGM) lion, roars before the feature starts, and there are serials on Saturday, including "Tarzan," "Buck Rogers," "Charlie Chan" and "Our Gang."

There are love scenes so tender, my mom would take a box of Kleenex to dry her tears. Nina Griner, the veterinarian's wife, bless her heart, enjoyed a good laugh. Actor Bob Burns blew his bazooka and rode the slow train through Arkansas.

Margaret Mitchell's "Gone with the Wind" enthralled capacity crowds. People even stood in the aisles. Walt Disney thrilled many a child and also adults with "Snow White and the Seven Dwarfs." Humphrey Bogart and Ingrid Bergman appeared in "Casablanca" on the same screen. We saw Pearl Harbor bombed, the battleships sinking in a cloud of black smoke to their watery graves. Yes, we could see it all for a few pennies. First, nine cents if you were under 12 years of age, then 15 cents. Thirty-five cents would admit an adult, now 50 cents. What are things coming to? I must have Charlie Chan and his Number One Son investigate these fare raises. Let's go. This is where we came in.

I do wish these young boys would quit throwing popcorn at groups of girls who are swooning when Frank Sinatra sings.

I might have amounted to more in life if that show hadn't been so close to my home. Why, it cost me 12 cents that Nick Pope had given me for fish wrapper newspapers or a fishing pole and a half that Eli Vickers had paid me for, of green bamboo. I should have saved my money instead of plunking it down in front of Miss Ida and having her pop a green paper ticket out that hole in the glass capsule that served as a cocoon against the public. If I had all that money back, I might even own my own picture show. Who knows?

Cast your view straight across Main Street over the plaza park, so worn by foot traffic. Not a blade of grass exists, except up close to the big oak trees that shade the park. There you will see Williams Chevrolet Co., founded by J. Gould Williams and his wife, Gussie. Chevrolets are popular cars. Some people swear by them. Others think Fords are the only car on the road. I would love to have either one. Some of Fitzgerald's finest gentlemen sell cars at Williams Chevrolet. Mr. J.C. Holder, Mr. W.C. Helton, Dude Floyd, Mr. E.C. Mann and Mr. Williams are all well acquainted with the public, a pleasure to trade with. No fly-by-night salesmen here.

Kathryn Hill—Mrs. Wiley Hill—was the head of the bookkeeping department. A Mrs. Biggers took her place until Thelma Griffin became head bookkeeper in the mid forties.

Roy Swanson is the head mechanic. Cliff Barronton and the Rodgers brothers are mechanics. Frazer Swanson and Bill Belvin are body repairmen who know no peer. There is a used car lot, occupied by trade-ins, that joins with the "side door" of Home Furniture Co.

Back on the west side of S. Main Street, on the alley, is a staircase leading up to the roof garden over the theatre. Special occasions are held here—dances and parties.

First across the alley is a furniture store, Cooks Furniture, operated by Randolph Cook, a semi-retired railroad conductor. He is a hometown boy. His father owned several buildings along here.

People live in apartments upstairs, mostly elderly people who have lived up there most of their lives. They come down in the evenings to visit and shop. Next is the Suwannee Store, a grocery chain with stores all over Georgia. They have a drink box and staple groceries and are a favorite of many farm people. Bob Millinor is the area manager. There is one just like this one on E. Pine Street. But I believe they are on their last legs as these supermarkets are catching on fast. At one time, Story Patterson had a very popular grocery in this building. Everyone liked Story and his wife, Iva Lee. He had too much credit out and failed. During the Depression, he opened several stores and made a good living, but none were as popular as his Vendome store, which for several years occupied this Suwannee store site. (The Suwannee Store was at 111 South Main.)

The next storefront is vacant, but after it is Echol Stone's grocery and meat market, run by Mr. Hughes and his hard-working young helper, Donald Leggett. Mr. Stone has many loyal customers who have stuck by him through lean and fat years, almost as well as those at Johnny Garrison's store. Hughes' meat market is probably the old line housewives' one and only place to buy meat. I see Armour's and Cudahy refrigerated delivery trucks backing up to the back door. The stout butcher man carries sides of beef—yes, whole halves of steers—into the "cold room," where Mr. Hughes and Donald break them down to go into the show case or to be custom-cut for the discriminating housewife or cafe chef. Lots of labor, but you know what you are buying. Return customers are the backbone of any business.

All good things must come to an end I have heard, many times. Fitzgerald certainly has not come to an end, only the day. We are back at Terminal Filling Station on the corner of Main and Central.

We have overlooked one of our citizens who has a small office in the rear of this station. He is Claude Jones, produce broker. Claude must have arrived here on a truck load of turnips from who knows where around 1945. He wears white shoes, a light-colored seersucker suit, white shirt, yellow tie and, always, that Panama hat. He's the only man in town with two telephones, a wire to the "spot" market and another one open for his customers. (A spot market is a market in which commodities, produce in this case, are bought and sold for cash and delivered immediately)

He has slips of paper stuck in his hat band, bearing

names and telephone numbers. His office equipment consists of a battered desk, where his feet rest as he relaxes in his swivel chair. Watermelons, cantaloupe, cabbage, kale, onions, you name it—Claude's eyes light up when a farmer drives up with a load of produce. Now, he is a big operator in watermelon season. He may buy and load dozens of railroad cars of melons, loaded on the team track just a block away, behind Asa Smith and Ralph Puckett's planer mill, SPS Lumber Company. (SPS Lumber Yard, owned by Asa Smith, Ralph Puckett and Asa Smith Jr., was located at 105 N. Main. They purchased rough lumber from saw mills, dressed it down to standard sizes and smoothed it.)

Scrap James loads the watermelons off mule-drawn wagons, old trucks or maybe a pickup truck. You might even see a Model "T" or Model "A" Ford. Now, Scrap has plenty of help. He only packs the melons, that is, beds them in oat straw so they can ride good, to Chicago or New York City.

Claude may drive up in his Chevy coupe to assure all the hands and growers that they will get their money tomorrow. He will spend hours, even days and nights, on those phones, calling all up and down the northeast coast, selling the produce to the markets. Somehow he manages to pay off. He is quite a character, single, and can move on short notice.

He had a date with "our" chemistry teacher, and we boys heard about it. One—I don't know who—drew a picture on the blackboard before she came to class of an engagement ring featuring 11 cabbages and one small diamond, under which were written the words "the engagement ring Claude Jones gave Miss Smith last night."

I see Claude is still around, telephone to his ear, fumbling for that pack of Lucky Strike cigarettes. One day he is very rich, the next he is broke. Hang on to those Lucky Strikes, Claude, or you may depart these parts on a rail, and I don't mean a railroad.

I haven't seen one of our most visible citizens on the street. He must be busy at the post office, where he is employed. His name is Wade Malcolm. He was in the Navy during the War and returned to become one of our first citizens. He is always building something—house, store, chicken coop. He loves to be a clown in a parade, anything for a laugh. Every year he is Santa Claus' number one representative. He reads children's Santa letters on the radio and ends every one with a "Ho, ho, ho." He isn't fat enough to look like Santa without a pillow stuffed in his shirt, but on the radio, it doesn't matter. I just didn't want us to miss him on this tour, because he loves this town.

We must be right on schedule, or pretty near, because I believe I hear the carillon chimes and the organ. Corinne Cannon, the talented organist, a protégé of Mrs. Perry's, is at the console. She is playing the "Bells of St. Mary's." No angel in Heaven can play sweeter music than Corrine. She plays at 5 p.m. on week days. The other musician, well known for her talent at the keyboard, is Polly Winn. She has a radio spot at noon, "Polly at the Piano." Great ladies, both a part of our uptown scene.

Now, go home and soak your aching feet. You should know your way around these old streets. If I have overlooked something or someone, come back tomorrow and we will take a second look. I probably won't be too far away, I hope. Love you all!

A word from the author.

This book would not have been possible without the encouragement of my wife Gladys, author Holly McClure, Editors Tim and Becky Anderson and staff from the *Fitzgerald Herald-Leader* newspaper, the Fitz-High Class of 1947, Professor John Barfield, Mrs. Frances Hiers, author Milton "Buddy" Hopkins, Margaret Hair, Jackie Harden, Mickey Foreman, Tony Sheppard, David Malcom, Margie Bryant, Janet Willingham, Peggy G. Luke, Emory Mann, Margaret Watkins, Mildred Evans Griffin, Martha Boggus, Patricia Walker, Anna Brown, author Erin Goseer Mitchell, the wonderful staff of the Fitzgerald-Ben Hill County Library, the untiring efforts of Sherri Butler, Features Editor for the *Fitzgerald Herald-Leader* newspaper, and my secretary Mariana Quiroga-Sasser, and my most esteemed publishers, Lee Clevenger and Preston Ward at ThomasMax Publishing.

Printed in the United States
35134LVS00006B/7-90